A NIGHT OF QUESTIONS—

ליל שאלות

הגדה של פסח

A PASSOVER HAGGADAH

EDITED BY

RABBI JOY LEVITT

RABBI MICHAEL STRASSFELD

ILLUSTRATED BY

JEFFREY SCHRIER

DESIGNED BY

ADRIANNE ONDERDONK DUDDEN

ליל שאלות
הגדה של פסח

A NIGHT OF QUESTIONS—
A PASSOVER HAGGADAH

THE RECONSTRUCTIONIST PRESS Elkins Park, Pennsylvania 5760 / 2000

PRAYERBOOK COMMISSION

Adina Abramowitz, Milton Bienenfeld, Rabbi Carl Choper, Rabbi Dan Ehrenkrantz, Lillian Kaplan, Marlene J. Kunin, Rabbi Mordechai Liebling, Leroy C. Shuster, Rabbi Reena Spicehandler, Jane Susswein, Rabbi David Teutsch (Chairman)

COMMENTATORS

Sylvia Boorstein, Rabbi Michael Cohen, Tamara Cohen, Rabbi Ira Eisenstein, Dr. Robert Goldenberg, Dr. Arthur Green, Rabbi Richard Hirsh, Rabbi Naamah Kelman, Dr. Lori Lefkovitz, Rabbi Barbara Penzner, Rabbi Sandy Eisenberg Sasso, Dr. Jeffrey Schein, Rabbi Toba Spitzer, Dr. David Teutsch, and Rabbi Sheila Peltz Weinberg

Library of Congress Number: 99-069556
International Standard Book Number: 0-935457-49-6

Hebrew Composition by El Ot Printing Enterprises Ltd (Tel Aviv)
English Composition by Duke & Company (Devon, PA)
Printed in the United States of America

In loving memory of Edith G. and A. Walter Socolow,
champions of Reconstructionism,
devoted parents and grandparents, and lovers of the family seder.

THE SEDER AT A GLANCE

CONTENTS

PUBLISHER'S NOTE

A Night of Questions is published by the Reconstructionist Press, a division of the Jewish Reconstructionist Federation. Also available from the Press are the *Kol Haneshamah* series of prayerbooks, books by the movement's founder, Mordecai M. Kaplan, and a variety of resources for educators. The JRF also publishes the magazine *Reconstructionism Today*. Founded in 1955, the JRF is the rapidly growing synagogue arm of the Reconstructionist movement. Currently numbering 100 affiliates, JRF congregations and ḥavurot are spread across North America. The JRF provides a wide array of services to its affiliates and is a voice of and for Reconstructionism in the larger Jewish world.

To order copies of *A Night of Questions* or to learn more about Reconstructionism, please contact:

Jewish Reconstructionist Federation/The Reconstructionist Press
Beit Devora
7804 Montgomery Avenue, Suite #9
Elkins Park, Pennsylvania 19027-2649
Phone: 215-782-8500 or toll-free 877-JRFPUBS
Fax: 215-782-8805
Email: info@jrf.org/Web: www.jrf.org

You may also wish to purchase copies of the CD/Cassette tape that accompanies *A Night of Questions*. It is recorded by *Shabbat Unplugged* and includes the liturgy of the Haggadah with both traditional and new melodies (indicated in the Haggadah by a musical symbol). It was produced by Rabbi Margot Stein and features Rabbi Micah Becker-Klein, Rabbi Myriam Klotz, Rabbi Rayzel Raphael, Juliet Spitzer, Rabbi Margot Stein, and Rabbi Shawn I. Zevit. For inquiries or to place an order, please contact the Reconstructionist Press at the above address.

PREFACE

WHY ANOTHER HAGGADAH? There are literally hundreds available, in every size and shape, written for every conceivable setting. The mandate to tell the extraordinary story of the Israelite Exodus is so strong, so powerful, and so important that each of us must try to do it in a way that connects the generations and speaks of the past to the future as though both were in the present.

That is what we have tried to do. We have created a Haggadah that is deeply rooted in the tradition of the Jewish people, responsive to those familiar with the tradition as well as to those whose connections to the tradition are just being made. We have tried to write a Haggadah that speaks to the "wise" child who has a thousand questions to ask, to the "wicked" child who stands alone and apart from the community, to the "simple" child who just wants to know why we keep telling this story, and to the child who does not know how to ask even the most basic of questions. This Haggadah is for all of us.

A Night of Questions carries on the tradition begun nearly sixty years ago, when *The New Haggadah*, edited by Rabbis Mordecai Kaplan, Ira Eisenstein, and Eugene Kohn, burst onto the American scene, making it the first liturgical work of the Reconstructionist movement. To say that it was radical is an understatement; its publication was nothing short of historic, as it reframed the whole nature of the observance of Pesaḥ by imbuing the seder itself with a sense of spiritual illumination the editors believed was missing from the traditional Haggadah.

The goal expressed by Mordecai Kaplan in 1941 rings true for this new effort as well. We hope to "articulate the prayer that is in the heart of every Jew, the prayer for a world which will be rid of all Pharaohs, and in which God alone will be sovereign."

ACKNOWLEDGMENTS

Many people nurtured this project to its creation. We thank the members of the Prayerbook Commission, whose names are printed on page 4, for their careful and thoughtful review of the text. We particularly acknowledge Mark Seal and Rabbis David Teutsch, Mordechai Liebling, and Richard Hirsh, who spent many hours with early drafts of the text and offered insightful and helpful comments.

We are grateful to the many colleagues who wrote commentary for *A Night of Questions* with wisdom and generosity. Their names can be found on page 4, their biographies on page 155. We thank the staff of Ma'yan: The Jewish Women's Project of the Jewish Community Center on the Upper West Side, and Dr. Gail Twersky Reimer of the Jewish Women's Archive, who, in an early meeting to discuss the Haggadah, suggested the idea of giving the Four Children an expanded role in the seder. Rabbi Susan Fendrick wrote the bibliodrama scenes and helped us, along with Dr. Lori Lefkovitz, develop the role of Miriam in the Haggadah. We thank Rabbi Lee Friedlander for his sensitive contribution of contemporary poetry and readings.

We were fortunate to work with two very talented people on the esthetic of the Haggadah: Jeffrey Schrier, whose extraordinary art is its own kind of midrash on the text, and Adrianne Onderdonk Dudden, who designed *A Night of Questions* with exquisite taste and never let anything faze her.

Fran Dunaisky, Sharon Dobbs, and Sylvia Jacobs graciously helped prepare the manuscript. Rabbi Judy Gary Brown, Dr. David Golomb, Phyllis Angel Greenberg, Amy Danto Hundert, Rabbi Reena Spicehandler, and Ruth Strassfeld spent many hours proofreading. Elliot Tepperman served as our production assistant. Lani Moss was our capable publisher's representative and Anna Rosenfield served as the administrative assistant.

We particularly want to thank our children: Sara and Ruthie Friedlander and Kayla, Noam, and Benjamin Strassfeld, who continue to ask the best questions. Finally, we thank the scores of friends, family, and colleagues who used early drafts of *A Night of Questions* at their Pesaḥ seders and shared with us their insights and suggestions in order to make it the Haggadah we really wanted to write.

Rabbis Joy D. Levitt and Michael J. Strassfeld, *editors*

INTRODUCTION

In every generation, each person should feel personally redeemed from Egypt, as it is said, "You shall tell your children on that day saying, 'It is because of what the Eternal One did for me when I went free out of Egypt.' For the Eternal One redeemed not only our ancestors; we were redeemed with them." (From the Haggadah)

The uniqueness of Pesaḥ is found in the notion, expressed in the Torah, that Jewish history is also a timeless present. Pesaḥ is not simply a commemoration of an important event in our past but an event in which *we* participated and in which we *continue* to participate. We are meant to re-experience the slavery and redemption that occurs each day of our lives. It is our own story, not just some ancient history that we retell at Pesaḥ.

To relive the experience, we are commanded to tell the story of the Exodus. As the Torah states: "Remember this day, on which you went free from Egypt, the house of bondage, how the Eternal One freed you from it with a mighty hand . . ." (Exodus 13:3). The focus for this reliving is the seder, when we gather together in families or groups to celebrate this ritual meal. The Hebrew word "seder" means "order," and the meal has a very carefully constructed order to it. The seder includes many rituals, such as eating matzah and *maror* (the bitter herbs), drinking four cups of wine, and eating a sumptuous feast. Its many symbols are meant to remind us, on the one hand, of the bitterness of slavery and, on the other hand, of the great joy of liberation.

In the midst of these rituals, we recite a special pedagogic and liturgical text—the Haggadah. Haggadah comes from the root meaning "to tell" and reflects the purpose of the evening—the retelling of the story of the Exodus. Celebrating the seder by reading the Haggadah is one of the most widely observed practices among Jewish people today. But underlying the fun and warmth of families and friends gathered together is an important religious drama in which the props are the symbols, the script is the Haggadah, and the actors are our families and friends.

Pesaḥ is the quintessential family holiday because of the importance it places in conveying the story and meaning of the Exodus to the next generation. It is the children's role to ask the Four Questions; it is our role to impress upon them the significance of the answers, for we understand fully what our children do not: that the future of the Jewish people lies with them. For that people to continue its 3,000-year history, each of us and each of our children must feel as though we ourselves were slaves in Egypt and were redeemed. In this way, each new generation can take its place in the chain of the Jewish people leading down from the Exodus to the present.

PLANNING YOUR SEDER

As you prepare for the seder, it will be helpful to keep in mind that if you try to read everything in the Haggadah, you will not finish the seder until morning, at the earliest! If that's what you (and your guests) want, fine. Otherwise, we suggest that you read through the Haggadah in advance and make decisions about what you wish to include. Remember: the mitzvah is to tell the story, not read the Haggadah. We've designed the Haggadah to be accessible on many levels and for many different kinds of seders—those with small children, older children, and adults only. We expect that, like the constellation of your families, your seder will look somewhat different every year—this Haggadah is intended to grow with you. Below are some general guidelines to help you prepare.

The Haggadah contains "text," which represents the core of the seder itself, along with *kavanot*, which are introductions to the text that are designed to set the tone for the text. *Kavanot* are indicated with the Hebrew letter KAF at the start of the paragraph. In addition, there are optional readings, marked with the symbol of a matzah at the beginning of the reading. There are marginal comments, reflecting a wide range of perspectives on the text of the Haggadah. Children who are readers should pay particular attention to the commentary designated with the symbol of four question marks. Parents who wish to engage children should look for commentary designated with the symbol of a kiddush cup. Finally, musical notes appear before songs and liturgy that have been recorded on an accompanying CD/Cassette recorded by *Shabbat Unplugged*. (For information about ordering musical CDs and/or tapes, please see page 8.)

We have designed several suggested seders in order to help you navigate the Haggadah. See "Parting the Waters" on page 157. The first is a seder that lasts approximately one and one-half hours before dinner and is intended for adults and children over the age of seven. Another seder is designed for adults and small children and should take about 45 minutes before dinner. A third seder is designed for occasions at which people of other religious traditions are participating. Finally, we have designed a fourth seder to highlight the feminist aspects of this Haggadah. Again, these are only suggestions. Feel free to use them in combination with one another or with other material in the Haggadah. When creating your seder, you may find it helpful to follow the outline listed on page 6.

There are several unique aspects of this Haggadah that may inform your decisions about what to include. A complete description follows. One key decision is how to tell the actual story of the Exodus. A full description of the various choices for the telling of the story follows.

UNIQUE ASPECTS OF THIS HAGGADAH

The Four Children The Haggadah speaks of four children — one wise, one wicked, one simple, and the one who does not know how to ask. In *A Night of Questions,* these children ask questions throughout the evening. Because we understand the four children as a reflection of four aspects of personality, we have given them a voice at the table. Of course, we have broadened our understanding of their characteristics. The wise child is also clever, insightful, thoughtful, intellectual; the wicked child is also challenging, alienated, demanding. The simple child is also direct; the child who does not know how to ask is also silent, bewildered. There are several ways to use the four children in this Haggadah. You can assign roles to various participants (though we strongly urge you to avoid typecasting your "wise" child as the wise child), or you can follow the questions of one of the children throughout the seder.

Miriam's Cup In recent years, many versions of the Haggadah have added various texts and rituals to the seder, incorporating the role that women played in the story of the Exodus. In this Haggadah, Miriam is introduced at the very beginning of the seder because she is such an important figure at the beginning of the story. A cup of spring water is placed prominently in the center of the table as the seder begins. It is discussed and its contents are sipped during the course of the seder.

The Blessings We have provided two different choices for every blessing, such as those over wine, *karpas* (green vegetable), and matzah. In addition to the traditional formula (**"Blessed are You Eternal One our God, sovereign of all worlds"**), we have included one that emphasizes the human role in blessing the source of life (**"We bless the spirit of the world"**). The phrase "spirit of the world" is unusual in the Hebrew *(ruaḥ ha'olam)* because it can carry both masculine and feminine verbs. We have used both in order to be as inclusive as possible. Sometimes we have included the alternative in brackets within the traditional blessing, while at other times the alternative stands as a separate blessing.

The Telling of the Story The core of the seder is the telling of the story. There are several different ways to approach this section of the Haggadah, allowing you to choose what feels most appropriate for your seder in any given year.

THE BIBLICAL TEXT

One of the most important innovations of the first Haggadah published by the Reconstructionist movement was that it placed the human heroes at the center of the story. This Haggadah continues that change from the traditional text in which God is the only central character. One option for the telling of the story is to read the biblical text, excerpted from the book of Exodus and adapted for the seder. It is found beginning on page 52. Below the text, you will find questions asked by the four children. You can read the text and their questions, assigning parts to seder participants. Or you can decide to focus on the questions of one child throughout this section. In the margin notes you will find answers to some questions, but you can generate your own answers around the table as well.

THE PLAY

Families with small children are encouraged to perform the skit found in Appendix I on page 146, which tells the story of the Exodus in an engaging way. Adults and older children can be the actors, while smaller children can use props, pantomime, and even costumes. Try to keep it simple; remember, just seeing their parents play Moses, God, and Pharaoh will enthrall most children.

THE BIBLIODRAMA

A third alternative is to act out one or more of the bibliodramas found in Appendix II on page 151. This technique enables participants to delve deeply into the story, role-playing a variety of scenarios. This technique is appropriate for adults and children over the age of seven. We have included an introduction to bibliodrama that provides guidelines to get you started. Those with a second seder may wish to do this on the second night.

FROM GENERATION TO GENERATION: THE STORY CONTINUES

Finally, particularly for those who hold two seders and want to do something different on the second night, the section entitled "*Beḥol dor vador,*" which is found on page 100, can be used as a way of "telling" the story. It focuses not on the Exodus from Egypt, but rather on the continuing story of exodus and liberation of the Jewish people, from ancient times to the present. This is a wonderful time to tell family stories of journeying to freedom and to explore other times in history when we as a people have experienced oppression and redemption.

A FEW OTHER HELPFUL HINTS FOR YOUR SEDER

ALTHOUGH MOST FAMILIES CHOOSE to celebrate the seder around the dinner table, this is not a requirement. Families with small children might consider holding the seder in a living room or den (with a floor covering to prevent stains from spilled wine or juice). This allows children (and adults) to feel somewhat less confined than they might at a dinner table.

A good way to keep the hunger pangs of both children and adults from abbreviating your seder is to put out several different kinds of hors d'oeuvres when you dip the *karpas* in salt water. The custom of dipping at the seder was probably borrowed from the Greek practice of serving hors d'oeuvres at lavish banquets. You can serve vegetables and various dips throughout the early part of the seder, though you'll want to make sure people have room for the meal.

You might ask participants in advance to be responsible for a specific section of the Haggadah. They can then make choices about which commentary and readings to use for a particular section. Be sure to let them know how much time they can take.

GETTING READY FOR PESAḤ

It is easy to lose sight of the main goal of Pesaḥ when you start actually preparing your house for the holiday. The meaning of Pesaḥ is not found in the act of removing *ḥametz* (leavened goods) though that process can involve us in the change that Pesaḥ brings into our lives. We eat or throw away or give away our old *ḥametz* to make room for the newness and sense of freedom that Pesaḥ brings. Participating in the removal of *ḥametz* helps us fully experience the festival. Pesaḥ brings a taste of freedom, declaring that we must give away or put away the normal, the routine, and try something different for a week. Then when we go back to the old and familiar, it may be transformed for us.

For a complete discussion on preparing your house for Pesaḥ, see the chapter on Pesaḥ in *The Jewish Holidays: A Guide and Commentary*, by Michael Strassfeld (Harper & Row, 1985). Below are some suggestions for getting your house ready for the festival.

1. Do a thorough cleaning of the house, with special attention to those areas where *ḥametz* might have been eaten or stored. Don't forget your car.
2. All *ḥametz* should be eaten, disposed of, or, if it is to be sold, put into separate cabinets or storage spaces. *Ḥametz* includes all leavened products, such as bread, pasta, and not-kosher-for-Pesaḥ cakes, cookies, and crackers. If you are in doubt, look for a label indicating the product is "Kosher for Passover." Items that do not need such a label include coffee and tea, sugar, eggs, meat, fish, fresh fruits and vegetables, and salt. By custom, Ashkenazic Jews do not eat legumes such as beans (although string beans are permissible), peas, lentils, rice, millet, sesame and sunflower seeds, and corn. Sephardic Jews do eat legumes. Many people wind down their purchase of *ḥametz* for a few weeks before Pesaḥ so there isn't a lot to manage. Others use this as an opportunity to make a trip to the local food pantry with any leftover (unopened) boxes of pasta, rice, bread, crackers, cookies, and the like. If there is still *ḥametz* that you wish to keep until after the holiday, you can arrange to sell it symbolically. Generally, this is done through your local rabbi.
3. Most dishes, silverware, pots, and other cooking utensils that are used during the year should be put away. Items that can be boiled can be made kosher for Pesaḥ. Clean out your refrigerator of all *ḥametz* and thoroughly wash it. Your oven, stove top, and sink will also need to be made kosher for Pesaḥ.

BEDIKAT ḤAMETZ
SEARCHING FOR *ḤAMETZ*

By the day before the seder your house should be pretty well ready for Pesaḥ. Soon after sundown on the night before the seder we conduct a final, mostly symbolic search of our homes for *ḥametz*. Many people hide a few slices of bread so that the children who participate in the search will have something to find. The search is done in the dark with a candle or flashlight and a feather to sweep up the crumbs. Before the search begins, recite the following blessing:

בָּרוּךְ אַתָּה יהוה אֱלֹהֵינוּ מֶלֶךְ הָעוֹלָם (נְבָרֵךְ אֶת רוּחַ הָעוֹלָם) אֲשֶׁר קִדְּשָׁנוּ בְּמִצְוֹתָיו וְצִוָּנוּ עַל בִּעוּר חָמֵץ.

Blessed are You, Eternal One our God, sovereign of all worlds (**We bless the spirit of the world**), who has sanctified us through the commandments, commanding us to remove all *ḥametz*.

After the search is complete, we recite the following:

כָּל-חֲמִירָא וַחֲמִיעָא דְּאִכָּא בִרְשׁוּתִי, דְּלָא חֲמִיתֵּהּ וּדְלָא בַעֲרְתֵּהּ, וּדְלָא יָדַעְנָא לֵהּ, לִבְטִיל וְלֶהֱוֵי הֶפְקֵר כְּעַפְרָא דְאַרְעָא.

All leaven in my possession that I have not seen or removed or of which I am unaware is hereby nullified and ownerless as the dust of the earth.

The next morning, the remaining crumbs are taken outside and burned; the formula recited after all the crumbs have been burned is:

כָּל-חֲמִירָא וַחֲמִיעָא דְּאִכָּא בִרְשׁוּתִי, דַּחֲמִיתֵּהּ וּדְלָא חֲמִיתֵּהּ, דְּבַעֲרְתֵּהּ וּדְלָא בַעֲרְתֵּהּ, לִבְטִיל וְלֶהֱוֵי הֶפְקֵר כְּעַפְרָא דְאַרְעָא.

All leaven in my possession whether I have seen it or not, whether I have removed it or not, is hereby nullified and ownerless as the dust of the earth.

פסח
זרוע
מרור
חרוסת

PREPARING THE SEDER TABLE

All of the objects on the seder plate are found in nature but also have a symbolic meaning. This illustration portrays the seder plate as if it were a vine, a living plant connecting the generations. Jeffrey Schrier

The preparation should involve the whole group or family if possible. Children can help set the table, color place cards, make matzah covers, and take charge of the salt water. The more people participate, the greater the sense of their involvement—and the lighter the burden on those doing the planning and cooking. In honor of the festival, and in celebration of freedom, many people set the table with their finest dishes. In honor of spring and the festival, some buy or pick flowers for the table.

In addition to copies of the Haggadah and whatever food will be served at the meal, the main items needed for the seder are the seder plate, *matzot,* wine or grape juice, salt water, and the cups for Miriam and Elijah. You will also need extra bowls of *ḥaroset, karpas,* and *maror.*

THE SEDER PLATE

THE SEDER PLATE CONTAINS all the symbols of the seder. While any dish can be used, many people own special seder plates with places marked for each item. One seder plate is enough, though some people provide more if the seder is very large. The items on the seder plate include:

1. *Karpas*—a vegetable, usually green such as parsley, symbolizing spring and rebirth. It is dipped in salt water near the beginning of the seder.
2. *Ḥaroset*—a mixture of chopped apples, nuts, wine or grape juice, and spices. The *ḥaroset* symbolizes the mortar that the slaves made for bricks in Egypt and is used to offset the taste of the bitter herbs. Recipes vary widely among Jews, though the above list is the most common among Ashkenazic Jews. Sephardic recipes often include figs, dates, raisins, and bananas as well.
3. *Maror*—the bitter herbs. Either romaine lettuce or freshly ground or sliced horseradish is used as a symbol of the bitterness of slavery.
4. *Beytzah*—roasted egg, symbol of the festival sacrifice. The egg should be hard-boiled and then, still in its shell, placed on a stove burner or in the oven until part of it is scorched.
5. *Zeroa*—roasted shank bone, symbol of the Pesaḥ sacrifice. The rabbis of the Talmud also allow a broiled beet, which is helpful for vegetarians.

Some seder plates have a sixth symbol, *ḥazeret,* additional *maror* to be used for Hillel's sandwich.

MATZOT THREE MATZOT, placed one atop the other, are used during the seder. They are customarily covered with a napkin or matzah cover and placed next to the seder plate. Use plain flour-and-water matzah for the seder, symbolizing *leḥem oni*—the plain bread of affliction.

WINE OR GRAPE JUICE FOUR CUPS OF WINE or grape juice are drunk during the course of the seder. The drinking of the four cups is a mitzvah, not an endurance test. Since it is important to be fully conscious at the seder, rather than sleepy or tipsy, you can alternate wine and juice or use only juice. If for reasons of health you cannot drink grape juice or wine, any other drink can be used.

SALT WATER BOWLS OF SALT WATER are placed on the table as a symbol of the tears of slavery. The *karpas* or green vegetable is dipped into the salt water early in the seder.

MIRIAM'S CUP AND ELIJAH'S CUP A LARGE GOBLET is set in the center of the table at the beginning of the seder, symbolizing the well of Miriam that sustained the Israelites during their journey in the desert. It should be filled with spring water. A large goblet is set aside for Elijah, who represents the longing for messianic days, which according to legend will be heralded by Elijah. Some legends hold that the prophet visits every home on Pesaḥ and drinks from his cup. Elijah's cup is filled by seder participants toward the end of the seder.

OTHER ITEMS FOR THE SEDER TABLE ***Pillows*** People use pillows to lean on whenever we are called upon to recline during the seder. The custom of reclining goes back to ancient times, when slaves ate standing up while free people ate while reclining.

Shemurah Matzah Some people use a special kind of matzah made from wheat that is "watched" *(shamor)* from the time it is harvested to prevent any contact with water that might cause leavening to ensue. Regular matzah is watched only from the time the grain is ground.

FOUR QUESTIONS TO ASK BEFORE STARTING THE SEDER

1. IS THIS STORY TRUE?

FOR GENERATIONS, Pesaḥ has been passed down as history: Moses, the ten plagues, the parting of the Sea of Reeds, the miraculous deliverance. Our ancestors recited the story of the Exodus to affirm their belief that it was true and to derive faith in the God who made it happen.

In our time, most of us tell the seder tale as sacred story rather than as historical record; we are skeptical of miracles; we are troubled by the moral implications of plague and punishment; and we seek a God commensurate with our enlarged vision of the liberation of all peoples.

Is this story true? No, not if we mean an accurate account of events that happened more or less the way they are told. But our ancestors, those who wrote the Bible and those who wrote the Haggadah, did not write history; they wrote of their experience of a Power greater than themselves that stood for freedom and against oppression.

They used mythic and poetic language, couched in the context of their world of experience. We do not live in that world, but we are the extension of the family that the Exodus created—the Jewish people. We do not tell the story of the Exodus because it is historically accurate; we tell the story because it is *our* story and we need to recover and uncover the eternal ideas that this story conveys. We take this story seriously but not literally. Pesaḥ is the way the Jewish people celebrate, affirm, wrestle with, and work for freedom as our human destiny.

2. WHAT KIND OF GOD IS THIS?

THE EXODUS STORY presents a conception of God that is both elevating and disturbing. In its setting, the story is not only about liberation: it is the breakthrough in history where a new idea of Divinity is advanced. This God is not a part of nature; rather, this God controls the natural world created by God. In the world of the Exodus, the deities of paganism are defeated—the Nile turns to blood; the sun-disk is obliterated; the Pharaoh is defied rather than deified. This God stands with the powerless and not with the powerful.

Yet this God also afflicts the innocent Egyptians (surely there must have been some innocent Egyptians); this God frees one people while visiting a night of terror on the first-born of another; this God "hardens the heart of Pharaoh" in order to lure his troops into a final crushing defeat amidst the waters of the Sea of Reeds. This God is called, among other things, a "man of war."

In order to uncover what lies behind these images, we need to remember that our ancestors bequeathed us both a conception *of* God and a belief *in* God. We are not beholden to their conception. It is mythic, legendary, and humanly constructed. It does not tell us much about God, but rather tells us what they believed God to be.

But as Jews we are beholden to, and bearers of, the faith that lies behind the story. The God of the Exodus story challenges tyrants, vanquishes adversaries, and liberates slaves. When the Israelites reached the safety of the far side of the Sea of Reeds and paused to look back, they did not say, "lucky break, low tide." They said rather, "This is God." That is where Judaism begins.

Whether there was a Sea of Reeds or not, our ancestors sensed a Power that makes for freedom, discovered in the moment of liberation and enshrined in the story and holiday that celebrates that freedom.

It is this God—the God that calls us to free the slaves, the God that stands against oppression, the God that continues to say, "Let my people go!"—it is this God in which we believe.

3. WHY CELEBRATE PESAḤ IF THE STORY ISN'T TRUE?

FOR THOSE OF US who find it hard to accept the story of Pesaḥ as historical truth and who struggle with the conception of God presented in the Exodus narrative, it is sometimes difficult to explain why we persist in the observance of this admittedly complex and demanding festival. We know that there are many Jews who have walked away from the experience of Pesaḥ and even from the orbit of the Jewish people.

Communities live through story and ritual. The great religious traditions seek, each in their own way, to address the fundamental questions of living: why are we here? What should we do? Think of religion as a conversation carried out over the centuries. Through holiday, ritual, story, and song, each religion calls together its community to encounter these eternal questions, generation after generation.

Pesaḥ is not "more true" or "better than" the festivals celebrating freedom found in other traditions, whether they be religious or secular. Pesaḥ is the way we Jews carry on our conversation about why we are here (to be free) and what we should do (serve God). Our rituals—the matzah, the *maror,* the salt water—are sacred not because "God said so" but because they are the symbols sanctified by thousands of years of Jewish history as the symbols that provoke our conversation.

Can a Jew have this conversation without Pesaḥ? Without the seder, matzah, the four questions? Jews can and Jews do. But if we want to have the conversation as Jews and with Jews, and if we want to mobilize our people, the Jewish people, to the work of freedom, it is to the seder that we come.

4. WHY IS THIS HAGGADAH DIFFERENT FROM ALL OTHER HAGGADOT?

A RECONSTRUCTIONIST HAGGADAH combines three imperatives:

1. It preserves as much of the mythic language, ritual, story, and song as is possible in order to help us join our lives to the story of our people.
2. It provides for and allows the most challenging, even radical questions about the historicity and content of the story to be expressed, wrestled with, and, it is hoped, resolved.
3. It tries to inspire us to seek the God who stands for freedom, and to become partners with God, the Power that makes for freedom, in enlarging the circle of liberation to encompass all peoples.

As you turn the pages of this Haggadah, you will step into the conversation of the Jewish people. We will indeed tell the story in the ancient words and celebrate the ancient (and contemporary) rituals. We are drawn into the story that is, after all, our story. No abstract discussion of freedom can compare to the power of the story of the Exodus.

This Haggadah will challenge you to ask questions, to consider replies, even to seek answers. We have tried to legitimate the daunting and often haunting doubts that many of us bring to the celebration of Pesaḥ, and to encourage you to allow these questions to surface.

This Haggadah will invite you to seek the God that challenges us, urges us on—let us say it directly: commands us—to seek freedom and to resist oppression. For Reconstructionism, however, this God is not a person, but a power and process making for freedom. While we do not literally believe that "God frees the enslaved," we do believe that freeing the slaves is godly. In a world where oppression still holds sway in so many places, affirming that faith becomes a holy task.

Richard Hirsh

הדלקת נר

CANDLELIGHTING

Jewish women have customarily followed the blessing of the candles with a *t'ḥine,* a private prayer, such as the following: May it be your will, my God and God of my ancestors, to be gracious to me and to all my family and to give us, and all Israel, a good and long life. Remember us with goodness and blessing, and grant us salvation and mercy. Grant us abundant blessing and fortify the places we call home. May your presence dwell among us as we gather here tonight. May we be blessed with wise and learned disciples and children, lovers of God who stand in awe of you, people who speak truth and spread holiness. May those we nurture light the world with Torah and good deeds. Hear the prayers I utter now in the name of our mothers Sarah, Rebekah, Rachel, and Leah. May your light reflected in these candles surround us always.
The Journey Continues (Ma'yan Haggadah)

We welcome the festival of Pesaḥ as darkness descends. As we kindle these lights, we remember that our ancestors discovered freedom in the midst of the dark final night in Egypt. Let the candles we now light be a reflection of the light that shines within each one of us, and let that light radiate throughout our home. We praise the Source of Light that keeps alive the hope of freedom amidst the darkness of oppression.

Light the candles and recite:

בָּרוּךְ אַתָּה יהוה אֱלֹהֵינוּ מֶלֶךְ הָעוֹלָם אֲשֶׁר קִדְּשָׁנוּ
בְּמִצְוֹתָיו וְצִוָּנוּ לְהַדְלִיק נֵר שֶׁל [שַׁבָּת וְ] יוֹם טוֹב.

Baruḥ atah adonay eloheynu meleḥ ha'olam asher kideshanu bemitzvotav vetzivanu lehadlik ner shel [shabbat ve] yom tov.

Blessed are you, Eternal One our God, sovereign of all worlds, who has made us holy with your *mitzvot* and commanded us to kindle the [Shabbat and] festival lights.

or

נְבָרֵךְ אֶת רוּחַ הָעוֹלָם אֲשֶׁר קִדְּשַׁתְנוּ בְּמִצְוֹתֶיהָ וְצִוַּתְנוּ
לְהַדְלִיק נֵר שֶׁל [שַׁבָּת וְ] יוֹם טוֹב.

Nevareḥ et ruaḥ ha'olam asher kideshatnu bemitzvoteha vetzivatnu lehadlik ner shel [shabbat ve] yom tov.

We bless the spirit of the world, who has made us holy with the *mitzvot* and commanded us to kindle the [Shabbat and] festival lights.

These lights remind me of the pillar of fire that guided the Israelites at night during the years of wandering on the way to the promised land. Just as that light brought the people together, we are now drawn together by the light of the Pesaḥ candles.
Michael Cohen

בָּרוּךְ אַתָּה יהוה אֱלֹהֵינוּ מֶלֶךְ הָעוֹלָם שֶׁהֶחֱיָנוּ וְקִיְּמָנוּ וְהִגִּיעָנוּ לַזְּמַן הַזֶּה.

Baruḥ atah adonay eloheynu meleḥ ha'olam sheheḥeyanu vekiyemanu vehigi'anu lazeman hazeh.

Blessed are you, Eternal One our God, the sovereign of all worlds, who gave us life, and kept us strong, and brought us to this time.

or

נְבָרֵךְ אֶת רוּחַ הָעוֹלָם שֶׁהֶחֱיַתְנוּ וְקִיְּמַתְנוּ וְהִגִּיעַתְנוּ לַזְּמַן הַזֶּה.

Nevareḥ et ruaḥ ha'olam sheheḥeyatnu vekiyematnu vehigi'atnu lazeman hazeh.

We bless the spirit of the world, who gave us life, and kept us strong, and brought us to this time.

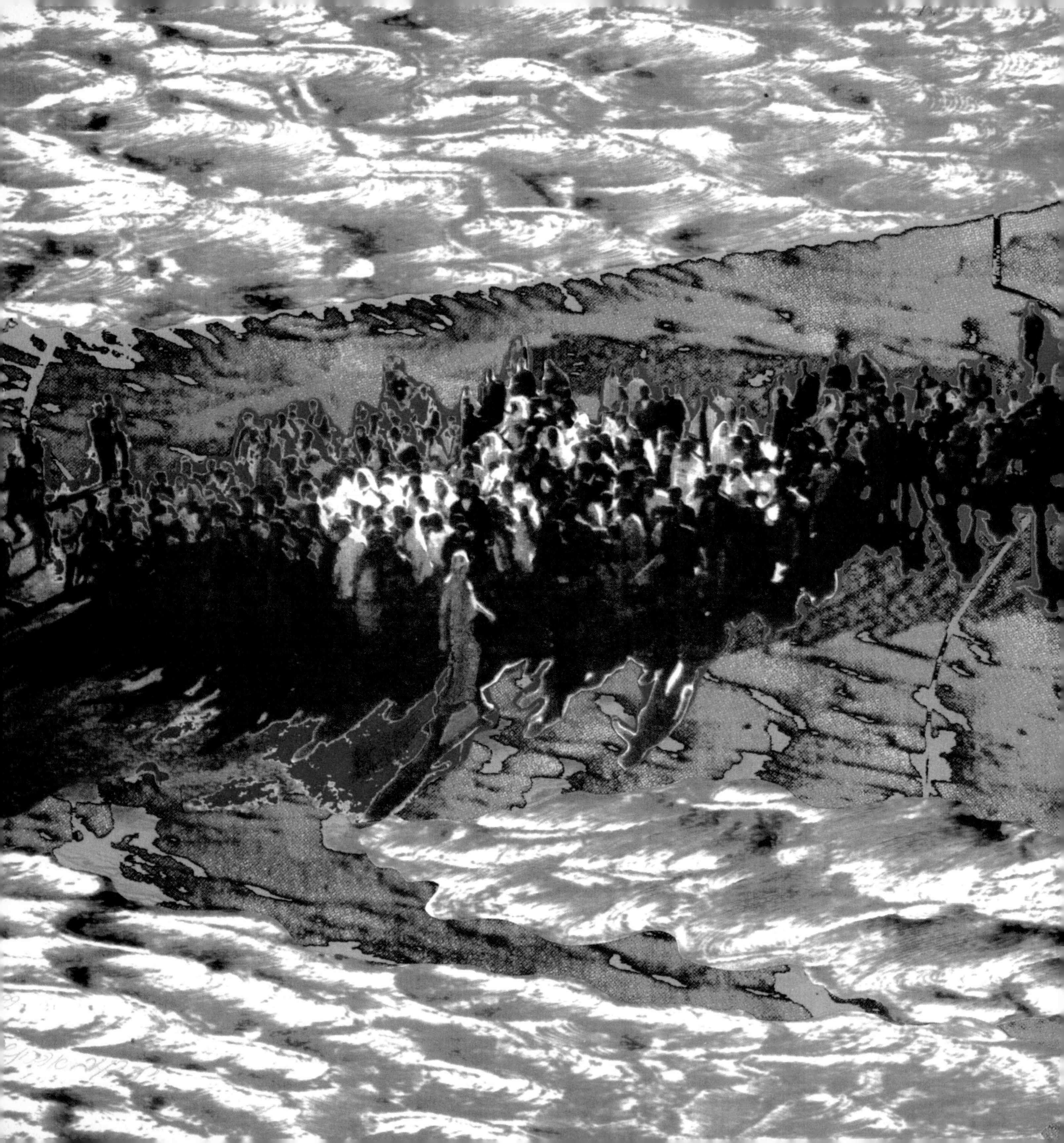

THE ORDER

קדש KADESH *blessing over wine or grape juice*

ורחץ UREḤATZ *hand washing*

כרפס KARPAS *dipping a vegetable in salt water*

יחץ YAḤATZ *breaking the middle matzah*

מגיד MAGID *telling the story*

רחצה ROḤTZAH *hand washing*

מוציא מצה MOTZI MATZAH *eating matzah*

מרור MAROR *eating bitter herbs*

כורך KOREḤ *eating matzah and* maror *sandwich*

שלחן עורך SHULḤAN OREḤ *the meal*

צפון TZAFUN *eating the afikoman*

ברך BAREḤ *blessings after the meal*

הלל HALLEL *reciting Psalms*

נרצה NIRTZAH *the conclusion*

The enduring reality of the Exodus has been apparent in our own time by the rescue of thousands of Ethiopian Jews who were flown to Israel in Israeli jets, finally safe from the danger of annihilation in Ethiopia. For the Ethiopians, lining up to board the planes was like stepping into the Sea of Reeds. Danger was at their backs, while both the promise of freedom and the fear of the unknown lay ahead. What other people have faced such choices? Jeffrey Schrier

OR GREAT SEA

JERUSALEM
Ashdod R.Jordan
Askelon Hebron
Gaza
CANAAN
Beersheba
Rhinocolura
Rehoboth
Eshcol

Nahaliel
Mattanal
Beer
Almon
Dibon
River
Zedek Zere

ta Mouth
tie Mouth
Port Said
Sin Pelusium
onis
hapanes
Suez
Succoth

WILDERNESS
ARABIA

Arabah

PENINSU
A MAP TO ILLUS
Wanderings of the
Canai

Huddah
Tahath
Hazeroth
Kibroth-Hattaavah
WILDERNESS
Rephidim
Mt Serbal
MT SINAI
EL HOREB
MT SINAI
GULF OF
MIDIAN
Desert of Shur
or Etham

GULF OF

Desert of Sin

INTRODUCTION TO THE SEDER

We begin our journey through the Pesaḥ seder, our journey from slavery to freedom. Through word and song, story and ritual, questions and more questions, we will relive the story of our ancestors' exodus and liberation.

We tell the story not only to preserve the memory. We tell the story because Egypt is not only one physical place. The Exodus was not just one moment in time.

We step into this story because it is both our story and the story of all people who have experienced oppression and liberation. When we recall the story of our oppression, we resolve to fight oppression everywhere. When we recall the story of our liberation, we renew our dream for freedom everywhere.

Tonight, we raise our voices as individuals and members of this seder community committed to marching together out of Egypt.

Miriam's Cup has become part of the seder ritual only in the last few years, but its origin lies in the midrash, which says that Miriam's well accompanied the Israelites through the wilderness until Miriam's death. Miriam, the sister of Moses, is thus associated with the ongoing redemption represented by water in the desert. In Miriam's Cup, filled with water, we have the parallel of Elijah's cup, which appears toward the end of the seder. But whereas Elijah stands for the redemption yet to come, Miriam reminds us of the redemption occurring daily in our lives. *David Teutsch*

Place Miriam's Cup, filled with spring water, on the seder table.

Even as we begin our story, we know its "end." Israel will leave Egypt and wander in the desert for forty years on the way to the promised land. According to legend, a well of water accompanied the Israelites on their journey in the desert.

This miraculous well was provided because of the merit of Miriam, the sister of Moses, who watched over her brother as he floated down the Nile, and later joined with him to lead the people across the sea. Tonight, we recall that well as we place Miriam's cup on our seder table.

In every generation, we experience both oppression and liberation. In our wanderings, both as a people and as individuals, Miriam's well still accompanies us as a sustaining presence in the desert, enabling us not just to survive, but to thrive.

Miriam's well reminds us that our journey has both direction and destination—to a place where freedom is proclaimed for all.

In this illustration, Miriam's well is represented by a water jug superimposed on a map. It is as though the sea itself was flowing from the mouth of the jug, which is held by graceful yet powerful hands. Jeffrey Schrier

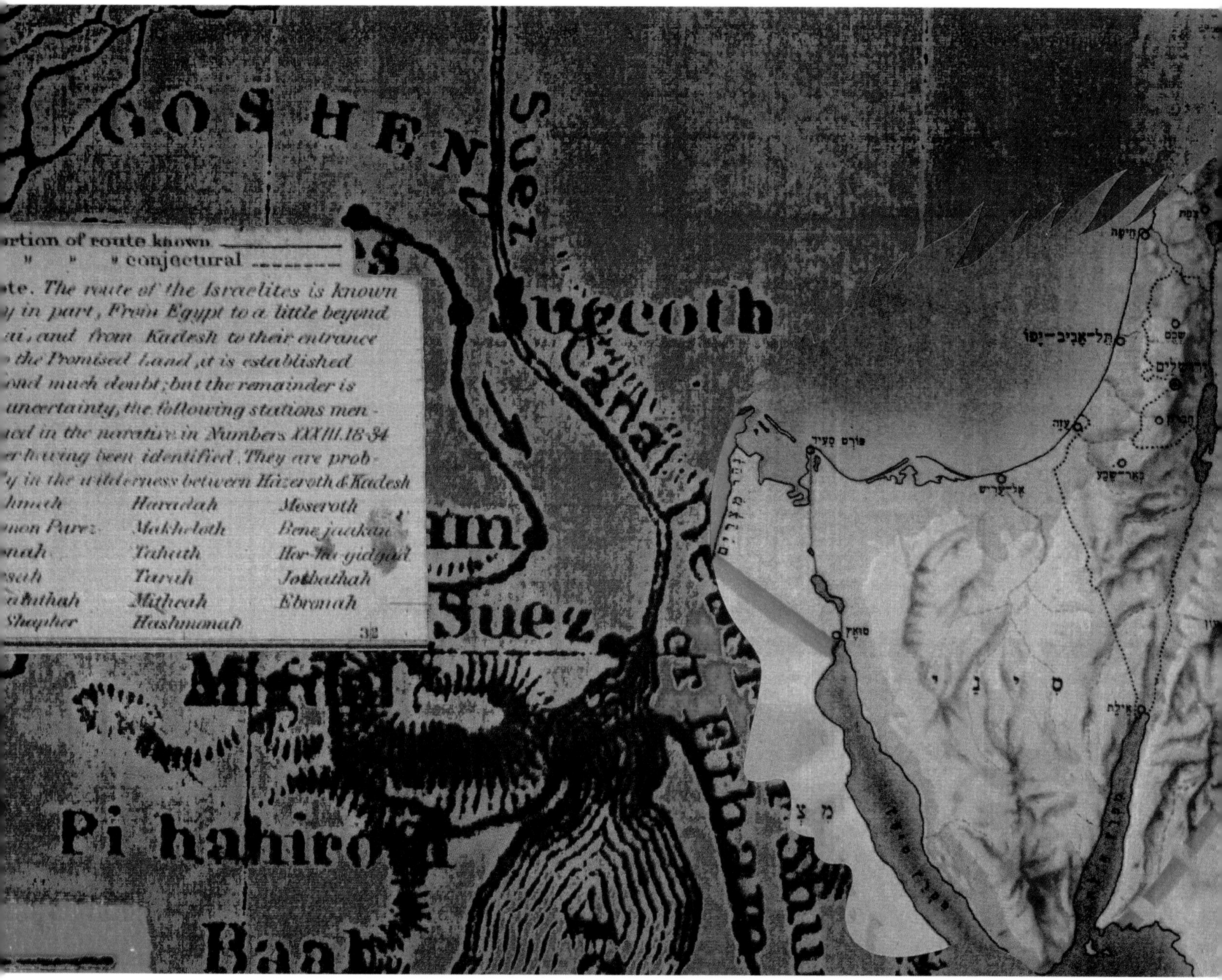
GOSHEN
Suez Canal
Succoth
Suez
Pi hahiroth
rtion of route known
» » » conjectural
te. The route of the Israelites is known
y in part, From Egypt to a little beyond
ai, and from Kadesh to their entrance
the Promised Land, it is established
ond much doubt; but the remainder is
uncertainty, the following stations men-
ned in the narative in Numbers XXXIII.18-34
er having been identified. They are prob-
y in the wilderness between Hazeroth & Kadesh
hmah Haradah Moseroth
mon Parez Makheloth Bene jaakan
nah Tahath Hor-ha-gidgad
sah Tarah Jotbathah
ahthah Mithcah Ebronah
Shepher Hashmonah
32
תל־אביב־יפו
ס י נ י

KADESH קדש

FIRST CUP OF WINE OR GRAPE JUICE

The process of coming to consciousness about our own enslavement is not always comfortable. It demands of us the courage to let go of a world view in which we are all-powerful and our problems are ones we could solve if only we could get it right. If only . . .

At first it may seem like admitting defeat to say that we are still enslaved. But it is exactly the opposite. Until an abused woman names her home Egypt, and until an abused employee names his work place Egypt, they will not leave. Until they see that their lives are connected to the lives of others, they will not break through their isolation and see their plight as part of a larger struggle. Many people choose to see their problems as personal weaknesses and defects rather than acknowledging that oppression still influences their lives. The Exodus could only have been a communal process. Seeing oneself as part of a larger whole is an essential step in breaking out of the isolation of enslavement.

Tamara Cohen

Tonight we will drink not one cup but four, as we recount the journey from exodus to liberation, a journey that stops in many places along the way. We come first to the recognition of slavery, of degradation, of narrowness. Until we know the ways in which we are enslaved, we can never be free. We drink this first cup in honor of awareness.

Recite on Shabbat. On weekdays, begin at the top of page 32.

וַיְהִי עֶרֶב וַיְהִי בֹקֶר יוֹם הַשִּׁשִּׁי:
וַיְכֻלּוּ הַשָּׁמַיִם וְהָאָרֶץ וְכָל־צְבָאָם. וַיְכַל אֱלֹהִים בַּיּוֹם הַשְּׁבִיעִי
מְלַאכְתּוֹ אֲשֶׁר עָשָׂה, וַיִּשְׁבֹּת בַּיּוֹם הַשְּׁבִיעִי מִכָּל־מְלַאכְתּוֹ
אֲשֶׁר עָשָׂה. וַיְבָרֶךְ אֱלֹהִים אֶת־יוֹם הַשְּׁבִיעִי וַיְקַדֵּשׁ אֹתוֹ, כִּי בוֹ
שָׁבַת מִכָּל־מְלַאכְתּוֹ אֲשֶׁר בָּרָא אֱלֹהִים לַעֲשׂוֹת.

[Vayhi erev vayhi voker yom hashishi:
Vayehulu hashamayim veha'aretz veḥol tzeva'am
vayeḥal elohim bayom hashevi'i melaḥto asher asah
vayishbot bayom hashevi'i mikol melaḥto asher asah.
Vayvareḥ elohim et yom hashevi'i vaykadesh oto
ki vo shavat mikol melaḥto asher bara elohim la'asot.]

[There was evening and morning, the sixth day. Heaven, earth, and all their beings were finished. God completed on the seventh day the work that had been done, and ceased upon the seventh day from all the work that had been done. God blessed the seventh day and set it apart. For on it God had ceased from all the work that had been done in carrying out Creation.]

Why does this illustration combine a human profile with a map of Egypt? When we try to locate Egypt—Mitzrayim—the narrow place—we might pinpoint different places in the world that are currently filled with strife. We might also see locations on maps that remind us of the history of our people's oppression. But narrow places are also inside each of us. As we gaze at the maps, we also need to search for that place within ourselves that causes us imprisonment and creates strife for others. That is why this illustration combines a human profile with a map of Egypt.

Jeffrey Schrier

Pesaḥ focuses on what can be called the "already/not yet" syndrome of Judaism. At our seder, we note a paradox: the festival celebrates freedom and redemption, and simultaneously reminds us that we are neither free nor redeemed! Pesaḥ is replete with perpetual tensions—between slavery and freedom, between redemption and exile, between homeland and wandering, between what has already happened and what has yet to occur.

Thus we open our seder with the words of the *Kiddush:* "this festival of *matzot,* the season of our freedom." But almost immediately afterwards, we uncover the matzah and recite: "Now we are enslaved, next year [may] we all be free." At the very beginning, the Haggadah articulates the paradox that will occur as a refrain several times throughout the seder—that while we are indeed "free" because of what happened back then, we remain enslaved until full liberation is achieved for all people. *Richard Hirsh*

Raise a full cup and recite, adding the [bracketed words] on Shabbat: The phrase (Nevareḥ et ruaḥ ha'olam) is an alternative form of blessing. *See page 13 for a full explanation.*

בָּרוּךְ אַתָּה יהוה אֱלֹהֵינוּ מֶלֶךְ הָעוֹלָם (נְבָרֵךְ אֶת רוּחַ הָעוֹלָם) בּוֹרֵא פְּרִי הַגָּפֶן.
בָּרוּךְ אַתָּה יהוה אֱלֹהֵינוּ מֶלֶךְ הָעוֹלָם (נְבָרֵךְ אֶת רוּחַ הָעוֹלָם) אֲשֶׁר קְרָאָנוּ לַעֲבוֹדָתוֹ וְרוֹמְמָנוּ בִּקְדֻשָּׁתוֹ וְקִדְּשָׁנוּ בְּמִצְוֹתָיו. וַתִּתֶּן־לָנוּ יהוה אֱלֹהֵינוּ בְּאַהֲבָה [שַׁבָּתוֹת לִמְנוּחָה וּ]מוֹעֲדִים לְשִׂמְחָה חַגִּים וּזְמַנִּים לְשָׂשׂוֹן אֶת־יוֹם [הַשַּׁבָּת הַזֶּה וְאֶת־יוֹם] חַג הַמַּצּוֹת הַזֶּה זְמַן חֵרוּתֵנוּ [בְּאַהֲבָה] מִקְרָא קֹדֶשׁ זֵכֶר לִיצִיאַת מִצְרָיִם. כִּי אֵלֵינוּ קָרָאתָ וְאוֹתָנוּ קִדַּשְׁתָּ לַעֲבוֹדָתֶךָ [וְשַׁבָּת] וּמוֹעֲדֵי קָדְשְׁךָ [בְּאַהֲבָה וּבְרָצוֹן] בְּשִׂמְחָה וּבְשָׂשׂוֹן הִנְחַלְתָּנוּ. בָּרוּךְ אַתָּה יהוה (נְבָרֵךְ אֶת רוּחַ הָעוֹלָם) מְקַדֵּשׁ [הַשַּׁבָּת וְ]יִשְׂרָאֵל וְהַזְּמַנִּים.

*Baruḥ atah adonay eloheynu meleḥ ha'olam (**Nevareḥ et ruaḥ ha'olam**) borey peri hagafen.*
*Baruḥ atah adonay eloheynu meleḥ ha'olam (**Nevareḥ et ruaḥ ha'olam**) asher kera'anu la'avodato veromemanu bikdushato vekideshanu bemitzvotav. Vatiten lanu adonay eloheynu be'ahavah [shabbatot limnuḥah u] mo'adim lesimḥah ḥagim uzmanim lesason et yom [hashabbat hazeh ve'et yom] ḥag hamatzot hazeh zeman ḥeruteynu [be'ahavah] mikra kodesh zeḥer litzi'at mitzrayim. Ki eleynu karata ve'otanu kidashta la'avodateḥa [veshabbat] umo'adey kodsheḥa [be'ahavah uveratzon] besimḥah uvsason hinḥaltanu. Baruḥ atah adonay (**Nevareḥ et ruaḥ ha'olam**) mekadesh [hashabbat ve] yisra'el vehazemanim.*

The use of the word "called" instead of "chosen" in the Reconstructionist liturgy should be viewed as a positive choice and not only as a substitute for the rejected concept of chosenness. We "hear" a call within the traditional forms of Judaism, including the seder, that addresses us on a profound level. The festival itself is called a *mikra kodesh,* literally a "holy calling," as though the day itself calls forth to us to respond. We do so by renewing our commitment to freedom on all levels, both for ourselves and for others. *Arthur Green*

Blessed are you, Eternal One our God, sovereign of all worlds (**We bless the spirit of the world**), who creates the fruit of the vine.

Blessed are you, Eternal One our God, sovereign of all worlds (**We bless the spirit of the world**), who has called us to your service, and made us holy with your *mitzvot,* and given us, Eternal One our God, in love [the Shabbat for rest], the festivals for happiness, the holidays and seasons for rejoicing, this day of [the Sabbath, and of] the festival of *matzot,* time of our freedom [with love], a holy convocation, a remembrance of the going-out from Egypt.

For you called to us, and made us holy for your service, and [with love and favor, the Shabbat and all] your holy Festivals, in happiness and joy, have given us, to have and to hand on. Blessed are you, Eternal One, (**We bless the spirit of the world**) who raises up to holiness [Shabbat,] the people Israel and their festive times.

The Torah refers to Nisan, the month in which Pesaḥ occurs, as the first month of the year—a kind of New Year. As people sit at the table, ask participants to share something new in their lives. *Naamah Kelman*

On Saturday night, insert Havdalah (p. 34) here. On each night, conclude the Kiddush *with the following:*

בָּרוּךְ אַתָּה יהוה אֱלֹהֵינוּ מֶלֶךְ הָעוֹלָם (נְבָרֵךְ אֶת רוּחַ הָעוֹלָם) שֶׁהֶחֱיָנוּ וְקִיְּמָנוּ וְהִגִּיעָנוּ לַזְּמַן הַזֶּה.

Baruḥ atah adonay eloheynu meleḥ ha'olam (***Nevareḥ et ruaḥ ha'olam***) *sheheḥeyanu vekiyemanu vehigi'anu lazeman hazeh.*

Blessed are you, Eternal One our God, sovereign of all worlds (**We bless the spirit of the world**), who gave us life, and kept us strong, and brought us to this time.

Drink while reclining.

We recline at the seder because in Roman times those who were free would eat while reclining (think of Cleopatra's couch as a typical dining room chair). On the other hand, slaves would eat while standing. The custom is to lean to the left on a pillow or the arm of your chair. We recline during the seder whenever we partake of a symbol of freedom (like wine or matzah).
Michael Strassfeld

On Saturday night, we recite a special version of Havdalah *at the end of* Kiddush, *distinguishing the sanctity of Shabbat from the sanctity of Pesaḥ:*

בָּרוּךְ אַתָּה יהוה אֱלֹהֵֽינוּ מֶֽלֶךְ הָעוֹלָם (נְבָרֵךְ אֶת רֽוּחַ הָעוֹלָם) בּוֹרֵא מְאוֹרֵי הָאֵשׁ.

בָּרוּךְ אַתָּה יהוה אֱלֹהֵֽינוּ מֶֽלֶךְ הָעוֹלָם (נְבָרֵךְ אֶת רֽוּחַ הָעוֹלָם) הַמַּבְדִּיל בֵּין קֹֽדֶשׁ לְחוֹל, בֵּין אוֹר לְחֹֽשֶׁךְ, בֵּין יוֹם הַשְּׁבִיעִי לְשֵֽׁשֶׁת יְמֵי הַמַּעֲשֶׂה. בֵּין קְדֻשַּׁת שַׁבָּת לִקְדֻשַּׁת יוֹם טוֹב הִבְדַּֽלְתָּ, וְאֶת־יוֹם הַשְּׁבִיעִי מִשֵּֽׁשֶׁת יְמֵי הַמַּעֲשֶׂה קִדַּֽשְׁתָּ. אֶת־עַמְּךָ יִשְׂרָאֵל קִדַּֽשְׁתָּ בִּקְדֻשָּׁתֶֽךָ. בָּרוּךְ אַתָּה יהוה (נְבָרֵךְ אֶת רֽוּחַ הָעוֹלָם) הַמַּבְדִּיל בֵּין קֹֽדֶשׁ לְקֹֽדֶשׁ.

*Baruḥ atah adonay eloheynu meleḥ ha'olam (**Nevareḥ et ruaḥ ha'olam**) borey me'orey ha'esh.*
*Baruḥ atah adonay eloheynu meleḥ ha'olam (**Nevareḥ et ruaḥ ha'olam**) hamavdil beyn kodesh leḥol beyn or leḥosheḥ beyn yom hashevi'i lesheshet yemey hama'aseh. Beyn kedushat shabbat likdushat yom tov hivdalta ve'et yom hashevi'i misheshet yemey hama'aseh kidashta. Et ameḥa yisra'el kidashta bikdushateḥa. Baruḥ atah adonay (**Nevareḥ et ruaḥ ha'olam**) hamavdil beyn kodesh lekodesh.*

Blessed are you, Eternal One our God, sovereign of all worlds (**We bless the spirit of the world**), who creates the light of fire.

Blessed are you, Eternal One our God, sovereign of all worlds (**We bless the spirit of the world**), who separates between holy and ordinary, light and dark, the seventh day and the six days of work. You separate between Sabbath holiness and Festival holiness, you set apart the seventh day from the six days of work, and you sanctify Israel with your holiness. Blessed are you, Eternal One (**We bless the spirit of the world**), who distinguishes among the kinds of holiness.

This is a special *Havdalah* since it marks the transition from Shabbat to a festival rather than from Shabbat to an ordinary weekday. The blessing over spices is therefore omitted. Since we just recited the blessing over wine, only the blessing for fire is recited, and we use the *Yom Tov* lights instead of a *Havdalah* candle.
Michael Strassfeld

URE̤ḤATZ ורחץ

HANDWASHING

There are several ways to accomplish this task. One person may walk around the table holding a pitcher of water over a basin, pouring a little water over each person's hands. All may visit a "washing station" set up near the seder table. A basin and pitcher may be passed around the table. In some families, one person washes on behalf of everyone. *Joy Levitt*

ב

We begin our story with the first stirrings of freedom. How was the desire for freedom first aroused? By the midwives, Shifrah and Puah, who resisted Pharaoh's decree to drown every Israelite boy in the Nile. By Miriam, who watched over her brother Moses to insure his safety. In the face of death, they advocated life.

In the birth waters and in the Nile, these extraordinary women saw life and liberation. Like the coming of spring, they believed in the inevitability of freedom and began the process of awakening their people. The waters of freedom open and close our story, taking us from the Nile to the Sea of Reeds.

Wash your hands. Since this washing is only symbolic, no blessing is recited.

Two remarkable women met by the water—Pharaoh's daughter and Miriam, the sister of Moses. The result of this interfaith encounter is the recovery of baby Moses and his royal "adoption." We do not know the name of Pharaoh's daughter, but we do know that she defied her father's evil decree and risked his wrath by taking Moses into her home. She and Miriam together began the cycle of love, hope, and ultimately, redemption. *Naamah Kelman*

KARPAS כרפס

DIPPING THE VEGETABLE

Karpas represents spring and new growth, rebirth and the beginning of new life. We taste in this fresh vegetable all the potential in nature and in ourselves. Tonight we celebrate our growth, the flowering of our spirit and of our voices.

We do not taste the vegetable alone. We dip it into salt water, recalling the tears our ancestors shed during their long years in slavery. We mix bitterness with sweetness, slavery with freedom, past with future. We live with the contrasts because we know that no moment exists without a multitude of combinations—sorrow and joy, pain and comfort, despair and hope.

עָנָה דוֹדִי וְאָמַר לִי קוּמִי לָךְ רַעְיָתִי יָפָתִי וּלְכִי־לָךְ. כִּי־הִנֵּה הַסְּתָו עָבָר הַגֶּשֶׁם חָלַף הָלַךְ לוֹ. הַנִּצָּנִים נִרְאוּ בָאָרֶץ עֵת הַזָּמִיר הִגִּיעַ וְקוֹל הַתּוֹר נִשְׁמַע בְּאַרְצֵנוּ. הַתְּאֵנָה חָנְטָה פַגֶּיהָ וְהַגְּפָנִים סְמָדַר נָתְנוּ רֵיחַ קוּמִי לָךְ רַעְיָתִי יָפָתִי וּלְכִי־לָךְ.

Arise my darling;
My fair one, come away!
For now the winter is past,
The rains are over and gone.
The blossoms have appeared in the land,
The time of pruning has come;
The song of the turtledove
Is heard in our land.
The green figs form on the fig tree,
The vines in blossom give off fragrance.
Arise my darling;
My fair one, come away!

Song of Songs: 2:10–13

Any vegetable can be used for *karpas*, though a green vegetable is preferred. The custom of using celery originated because the word *karpas* is related to the Persian and Aramaic word *karafas*, meaning celery. Scholars speculate that the practice of dipping goes back to ancient Roman banquet customs that began a meal with various hors d'oeuvres.

Many people like to use potatoes, in a way the simplest of all foods. Potatoes were given to Ethiopian Jews as their first meal upon their arrival in Israel so that their bodies, racked with hunger from years of subsistence living and months of starvation during their long trek toward freedom, would not be subjected to the shock of rich food. In the experience of Ethiopian Jewry, the story of the Exodus has been reenacted in our own day.
Michael Strassfeld

How do you know when springtime is here? How many symbols of spring can you find on the seder table? What symbols of spring can you find outside?
Joy Levitt

Dip a vegetable in salt water and recite:

בָּרוּךְ אַתָּה יהוה אֱלֹהֵינוּ מֶלֶךְ הָעוֹלָם בּוֹרֵא פְּרִי הָאֲדָמָה.

Baruḥ atah adonay eloheynu meleḥ ha'olam borey peri ha'adamah.

Blessed are you, Eternal One our God, sovereign of all worlds, who creates fruit of the earth.

or

נְבָרֵךְ אֶת רוּחַ הָעוֹלָם בּוֹרֵאת פְּרִי הָאֲדָמָה.

Nevareḥ et ruaḥ ha'olam boreyt peri ha'adamah.

We bless the spirit of the world, who creates fruit of the earth.

Eat the vegetable.

It is a custom in some families to plant parsley seeds on Tu BiShevat, the New Year of the Trees, which then grow into the parsley that is used at the seder. The renewal of the earth in springtime reminds us of the remarkable power of nature to renew itself. Pesaḥ is a time to marvel at and celebrate this potential intrinsic in all life.
Sheila Peltz Weinberg

Overleaf:
Broken fragments of matzah are like pieces of a puzzle in this illustration. Some segments depict the bread of affliction while others represent the journey and destination of the Israelites. Perhaps the piece of matzah may be seen as the unknown pieces of ourselves that, when known and understood, carry us forward toward a worthwhile destination. Putting together our "pieces" can be a kind of tikun*—a repair.* *Jeffrey Schrier*

The seder includes numerous contrasting symbols: parsley in salt water and bitter *maror* in sweet *ḥaroset;* death in the shank bone next to the egg of life on the seder plate; matzah both as a symbol of freedom and bread of affliction. What is the connection between these contradictions and freedom?

Human beings are deeply conditioned to crave the pleasant and the sweet and avoid the unpleasant. This is a natural tendency. However, to be free means relating fully to all experience and choosing how to act because we wish to realize our values and commitments.

As free beings tonight we embrace all experience and are not shaken or driven by our fears and desires to make our experience conform to our expectations. We are free insofar as we do not automatically identify pleasant and unpleasant with good and bad, with desirable and undesirable, with true and false. Freedom entails a perspective that is wider than our likes and dislikes. *Sheila Peltz Weinberg*

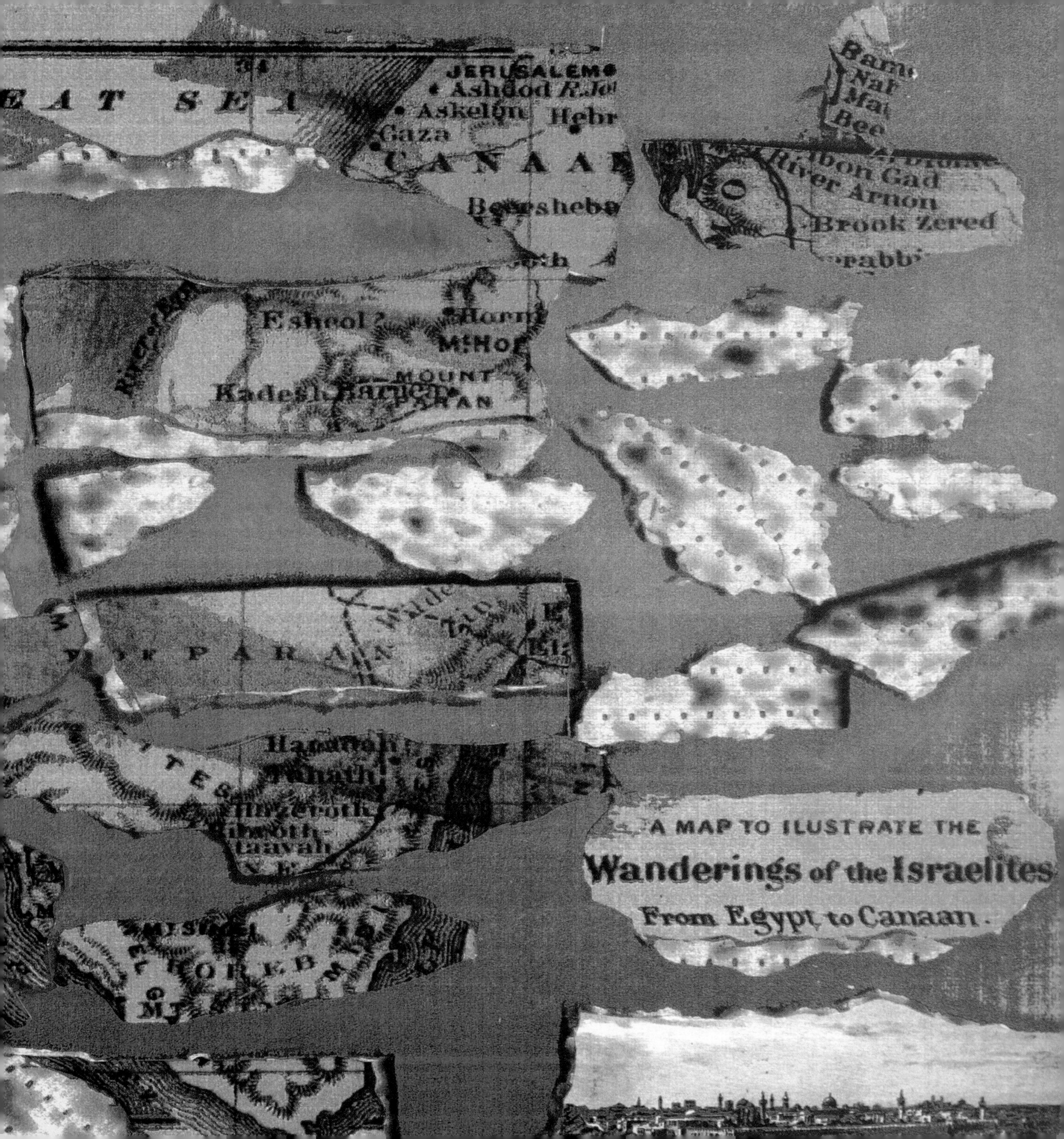
JERUSALEM
Ashdod
Askelon
Gaza
CANAA
Beersheba
River Arnon
Brook Zered
Eshcol
Kadesh
MOUNT
PARAN
PARAN
Hazeroth
HOREB
A MAP TO ILUSTRATE THE
Wanderings of the Israelites
From Egypt to Canaan.

MEDITERRA
AN OR G
Damietta Mouth
Damietta
The route of the Israelites is know
in part, From Egypt to a little beyo
, and from Kadesh to their entran
he Promised Land, it is establishe

YAḤATZ יחץ

BREAKING THE MIDDLE MATZAH

The most common explanation for *yaḥatz* links the breaking of the matzah to the term *leḥem oni*. The word *oni* can be translated as "the bread of affliction," thereby expressing the notion of matzah as a symbol of the poor fare we were given as slaves in Egypt. The symbol of even that simplest fare is broken in half to stress the extreme poverty of our lives in Egypt. *Oni* can also be translated as "the bread over which much is answered," pointing to the matzah that lies before us as we discuss and ask questions concerning the Exodus. *Michael Strassfeld*

Take the middle matzah and break it into two pieces. Wrap the larger piece in a napkin and set it aside. It will be the afikoman. *Place the smaller piece between the other two* matzot.

Choose one of the following readings:

No prayer is recited before we break the middle matzah on our seder plate. This is a silent act. We realize that, like the broken matzah, we are all incomplete, with prayers yet to be fulfilled, promises still to be redeemed.

We hide part of this broken matzah and hope it will be found by the end of our seder meal, for we recognize that parts of ourselves are yet unknown. We are still discovering what makes us whole.

We hide the larger of the two parts of the middle matzah because we know that more is hidden than is revealed.

We prepared for Pesaḥ in the night, searching for the hidden leavened bread; we will end the seder in the night, searching for the unleavened bread.

With the generations that have come before us and with one another, our search begins.

Harold Schulweis

The ritual challenge for children is to find the *afikoman*, but there can be an ethical challenge as well. Hide *tzedakah* certificates to various organizations that help the poor. After Pesaḥ, kids can redeem the certificates for checks to be sent to each organization in order to fulfill the mitzvah, "Let all who are hungry come and eat." *Jeffrey Schein*

???

Keep your eyes on the seder leader, who has just broken the middle matzah. Sometime, probably soon, he or she will hide it. Your job will be to find it and to bargain for its return with the one who hid it in the first place. This is an important job. Unless and until the leader has the *afikoman*, the seder cannot be completed. Work in teams and make your deal on behalf of all the children—it's more fun that way. *Joy Levitt*

Some do not get the chance to rise like golden loaves of *ḥallah*, filled with sweet raisins and crowned with shiny braids.

Rushed, neglected, not kneaded by caring hands, we grow up afraid that any touch might cause a break. There are some ingredients we never receive.

Tonight, let us bless our cracked surfaces and sharp edges, unafraid to see our brittleness and brave enough to see our beauty.

Reaching for wholeness, let us piece together the parts of ourselves we have found, and honor all that is still hidden.

Tamara Cohen

Our family's custom is to hide a piece of the *afikoman* for each child in an envelope marked with that child's name on it. The children then search for their envelopes, with the older children helping the younger ones. This eliminates competition, encourages cooperation, and keeps everyone happy. *Mickey Bienenfeld*

MAGID מַגִּיד

TELLING THE STORY

Uncover the matzot.

הָא לַחְמָא עַנְיָא דִּי אֲכַלוּ אַבְהָתַֽנָא בְּאַרְעָא דְמִצְרָֽיִם. כָּל־דִּכְפִין יֵיתֵי וְיֵיכֻל, כָּל־דִּצְרִיךְ יֵיתֵי וְיִפְסַח. הָשַׁתָּא הָכָא, לְשָׁנָה הַבָּאָה בְּאַרְעָא דְיִשְׂרָאֵל. הָשַׁתָּא עַבְדֵי, לְשָׁנָה הַבָּאָה בְּנֵי חוֹרִין.

This is the bread of our poverty, which our ancestors ate in the land of Egypt. Let all who are hungry come and eat. Let all who are in need come and celebrate Pesaḥ. Now we are here—next year in the land of Israel. Now we are slaves. Next year we will be free.

As we invite all who are hungry, we symbolically include all who are oppressed throughout the world.

יְהִי רָצוֹן מִלְּפָנֶֽיךָ יהוה אֱלֹהֵֽינוּ וֵאלֹהֵי אֲבוֹתֵֽינוּ כְּשֵׁם שֶׁלָּקַֽחְתָּ גּוֹי מִקֶּֽרֶב גּוֹי וְהֶעֱבַֽרְתָּ אֶת־עַמְּךָ יִשְׂרָאֵל בְּתוֹךְ הַיָּם, כֵּן תְּרַחֵם עַל אַחֵֽינוּ כָּל־בֵּית יִשְׂרָאֵל וְכָל יוֹשְׁבֵי תֵּבֵל (וּבִפְרַט...) הַנְּתוּנִים בְּצָרָה וּבְשִׁבְיָה, הָעוֹמְדִים בֵּין בַּיָּם וּבֵין בַּיַּבָּשָׁה. תַּצִּילֵם וְתוֹצִיאֵם מִצָּרָה לִרְוָחָה וּמֵאֲפֵלָה לְאוֹרָה וּמִשִּׁעְבּוּד לִגְאֻלָּה, בִּמְהֵרָה בְיָמֵֽינוּ וְנֹאמַר אָמֵן.

May it be your will, Eternal One our God and God of our ancestors, that just as you took the Israelites from among the Egyptians and led them through the sea, so may you have mercy on those among the House of Israel and among all peoples (especially . . .) who are distressed and oppressed, whether on land or sea. Save them and take them from the narrow straits to abundant favor, from darkness to light, and from enslavement to redemption, speedily in our days and let us say: Amen.

The phrase "now we are slaves" sets up the dramatic tension that embraces the entire seder. On the one hand we are proclaiming, "Thank God we are free!" and we soon say, "We were slaves to Pharaoh in Egypt . . . and had God not taken our ancestors out of Egypt, we . . . would still be enslaved." Liberation happened long ago, and as good, faithful Jews we still remember it. But here we say the opposite: We are still slaves! Our liberation never quite succeeded. This seder is about present and future liberation, not only that of the past. We still need to come forth from Egypt.

Both of these versions of liberation are true. When seen from the viewpoint of our one-time total bondage and that of Jews and others within our own memory, we indeed have every reason to be grateful. But the human condition is such that we still struggle to be free. Conversation at the seder table should attempt to encompass both of these truths. *Arthur Green*

Ha laḥma anya probably originated during a period when Aramaic was the spoken language of the Jewish community. Rashi makes the point that using the vernacular at this important moment of the seder reminds us how important it is to welcome people in a language that they can understand. *Joy Levitt*

Whom could we imagine inviting to the seder this year? Who in our lives, in our neighborhoods, in our world, is a victim of oppression? Go around the table naming those whom we ought to invite to the seder. *Michael Strassfeld*

We understand the invitation to include "all who are hungry," but why then does the Haggadah add the words, "all who are in need"? Perhaps the second phrase refers to those who would be alone at the seder.

Having suffered affliction ourselves, we should be more sensitive to the needs of others. So the seder begins with a reminder to care for others through *tzedakah* and *haḥnasat orḥim,* inviting others who are lacking to come partake in the festive meal. *Michael Cohen*

FOUR QUESTIONS

Each Pesaḥ, the four questions asked by the youngest child are exactly the same. Why do we ask them year after year? Because as we grow and change, our questions take on new meanings, and the answers to them differ. Because as we grow and change, we understand that there is no one right answer. Because as we grow and change, a different one among us may be asking the questions for the first time.

To ask questions is to acknowledge first and foremost that we do not live in isolation, that we need each other. To ask questions is to signal our desire to grow. By admitting what we do not know, we take the first steps toward greater knowledge and learning. To ask questions is to signify our freedom.

Fill the second cup.

There are many different versions of the Four Questions, which were in fact never meant to be anything more than examples of questions that could be asked. The Talmud tells a story to emphasize this point. A student, Abaye, was at the seder of his teacher, Rabbah. Some time during the early part of the seder, Rabbah had all the dishes, including the seder plate, cleared from the table. "Why are you clearing the seder plate from the table when we haven't even eaten the meal?" Abaye asked. (Some *Haggadot* instruct us to remove the seder plate here in order to provoke this very question.)

According to the Talmud, Rabbah responded that Abaye's question was the equivalent of the *Mah Nishtanah*, which now did not need to be recited (Pesaḥim 115b). So we learn that the goal of the evening is to ask questions, particularly new and different questions.
Michael Strassfeld

Why do we fill our cups now? Won't we be tempted to drink too early? This full cup is the witness to the story of the Exodus. It will be raised in honor of the greatness of the liberation and it will be spilled in memory of those who suffered in the process. When the time comes to drink it, we will know not only the joy of freedom, but we will know the price of our freedom as well. This cup begins with joy and ends with compassion. *Barbara Penzner*

If anyone at the table does not understand Hebrew, the Four Questions must be translated. In the Yemenite ritual, a child recites a short version of the entire Haggadah in Judeo-Arabic. Our family's custom is to ask people to recite the Four Questions in their native language. *Mordechai Liebling*

מַה נִּשְׁתַּנָּה הַלַּיְלָה הַזֶּה מִכָּל־הַלֵּילוֹת!

שֶׁבְּכָל־הַלֵּילוֹת אָנוּ אוֹכְלִין חָמֵץ וּמַצָּה,
הַלַּיְלָה הַזֶּה כֻּלּוֹ מַצָּה.

שֶׁבְּכָל־הַלֵּילוֹת אָנוּ אוֹכְלִין שְׁאָר יְרָקוֹת,
הַלַּיְלָה הַזֶּה מָרוֹר.

שֶׁבְּכָל־הַלֵּילוֹת אֵין אָנוּ מַטְבִּילִין אֲפִילוּ פַּעַם אֶחָת,
הַלַּיְלָה הַזֶּה שְׁתֵּי פְעָמִים.

שֶׁבְּכָל־הַלֵּילוֹת אָנוּ אוֹכְלִין בֵּין יוֹשְׁבִין וּבֵין מְסֻבִּין,
הַלַּיְלָה הַזֶּה כֻּלָּנוּ מְסֻבִּין.

Pesaḥ gave the Jews, through the ritual of the seder, a lesson in education. It is a lesson to the Jewish people, intended to point to the spirit in which a person must learn to educate the young. If we study the seder from that standpoint, we note that it is intended to serve as a token of three important principles: First, that education can and should constitute a religious experience. Second, the parental responsibility for the education of the child should be prior to that of the state. Third, the most important training should be training in freedom. *Mordecai M. Kaplan, adapted*

Language can be very powerful. At my family's seder, our custom is to go around the table, reading in both English and Hebrew. When my grandmother was alive, she always asked the next person to read when it was her turn, claiming that she had forgotten her glasses. Even as a young child, I sensed her embarrassment at reading in public in a language that wasn't her first tongue.

One year, I brought my college roommate home for the seder. A Russian major, she began to speak with my grandmother in Russian, and soon my grandmother was quoting Pushkin by heart. This woman whom I had believed to be illiterate was finally able to give voice to memories of her childhood that she had buried in order to be an American.
Joy Levitt

Mah nishtanah halaylah hazeh mikol haleylot!
Shebeḥol haleylot anu oḥlin ḥametz umatzah,
Halaylah hazeh kulo matzah.
Shebeḥol haleylot anu oḥlin she'ar yerakot,
Halaylah hazeh maror.
Shebeḥol haleylot eyn anu matbilin afilu pa'am eḥat,
Halaylah hazeh shetey fe'amim.
Shebeḥol haleylot anu oḥlin beyn yoshvin uveyn mesubin
Halaylah hazeh kulanu mesubin.

Why is this night different from all other nights?

On all other nights we eat leavened or unleavened bread.
Why on this night do we eat only matzah?

On all other nights we eat various kinds of vegetables.
Why on this night do we eat bitter herbs?

On all other nights we need not dip our vegetables even once.
Why on this night do we dip them twice?

On all other nights we eat either sitting up or reclining.
Why on this night do we eat reclining?

The whole point of the seder is to ask questions. This is your time to ask about things that confuse you, things you don't understand, or even things you don't agree with. There really is no such thing as a stupid question, especially tonight.
Joy Levitt

THE FOUR QUESTIONS

Why is it only on Passover night
we never know how to do anything right?
We don't eat our meals in the regular ways,
the ways that we do on all other days.
Cause on all other nights we may eat
all kinds of wonderful good bready treats,
like big purple pizza that tastes like a pickle,
crumbly crackers and pink pumpernickel,
sassafras sandwich and tiger on rye,
fifty felafels in pita, fresh-fried.
With peanut butter and tangerine sauce
spread onto each side up-and-down, then across,
and toasted whole-wheat bread with liver and ducks,
and crumpets and dumplings, and bagels and lox,
and doughnuts with one hole and doughnuts with four,
and cake with six layers and windows and doors.
Yes—on all other nights we eat all kinds of bread,
but tonight of all nights we munch matzah instead.

And on all other nights we devour
vegetables, green things, and bushes and flowers,
lettuce that's leafy and candy-striped spinach,
fresh silly celery (Have more when you're finished!)
Cabbage that's flown from the jungles of Glome
by a polka-dot bird who can't find his way home,
daisies and roses and inside-out grass
and artichoke hearts that are simply first-class!
Sixty asparagus tips served in glasses
with anchovy sauce and some sticky molasses.
But on Passover night you would never consider
eating an herb that wasn't all bitter.

And on all other nights you would probably flip
if anyone asked you how often you dip.
On some days I only dip one Bup-Bup egg
in a teaspoon of vinegar mixed with nutmeg,
but sometimes we take more than ten thousand tails
of the Yakkity-birds that are hunted in Wales,
and dip them in vats full of Mumbegum juice.
Then we feed them to Harold, our six-legged moose.
Or we don't dip at all! We don't ask your advice.
So why on this night do we have to dip twice?

And on all other nights we can sit as we please,
on our heads, on our elbows, our backs or our knees,
or hang by our toes from the tail of a Glump
or on top of a camel with one or two humps,
with our foot on the table, our nose on the floor,
with one ear in the window and one out the door,
doing somersaults over the greasy k'nishes
or dancing a jig without breaking the dishes.
Yes—on all other nights you sit nicely when dining,
So why on this night must it all be reclining?

Eliezer Lorne Segal

Can you find the funny things in the illustration that are mentioned in the poem?
Jeffrey Schrier

It is in the telling that transformation occurs. In every liberation movement, the sharing of stories becomes crucial. When women first gathered in consciousness raising groups or alcoholics shared their "experience, strength, and hope" in smoky church basements, stories were shared. I begin to see that my story isn't just my story. First we touch the common pain, then the common hope. From there we devise strategies for transformation. I am no longer caught in the isolation of my uniqueness. The fear and self-doubt that I feel about myself is revealed to be without substance. Every oppressor knows how subversive groups can be and tries to keep the oppressed from talking to each other, from telling their stories to one another. *Sheila Peltz Weinberg*

How do we begin the story? The Talmud presents two views. The rabbinic sage Samuel began with physical enslavement:

עֲבָדִים הָיִינוּ לְפַרְעֹה בְּמִצְרָיִם. וַיּוֹצִיאֵנוּ יהוה אֱלֹהֵינוּ מִשָּׁם בְּיָד חֲזָקָה וּבִזְרוֹעַ נְטוּיָה. וְאִלּוּ לֹא הוֹצִיא הַקָּדוֹשׁ בָּרוּךְ הוּא אֶת־אֲבוֹתֵינוּ מִמִּצְרַיִם, הֲרֵי אָנוּ וּבָנֵינוּ וּבְנֵי בָנֵינוּ מְשֻׁעְבָּדִים הָיִינוּ לְפַרְעֹה בְּמִצְרָיִם. וַאֲפִלּוּ כֻּלָּנוּ חֲכָמִים, כֻּלָּנוּ נְבוֹנִים, כֻּלָּנוּ זְקֵנִים, כֻּלָּנוּ יוֹדְעִים אֶת־הַתּוֹרָה, מִצְוָה עָלֵינוּ לְסַפֵּר בִּיצִיאַת מִצְרָיִם. וְכָל־הַמַּרְבֶּה לְסַפֵּר בִּיצִיאַת מִצְרַיִם הֲרֵי זֶה מְשֻׁבָּח.

We were slaves to Pharaoh in Egypt. The Eternal One our God brought us out from there with a strong hand and an outstretched arm. Had God not taken our ancestors out of Egypt, then we and our children and our children's children would still be enslaved to Pharaoh in Egypt. And even if all of us were wise scholars, all of us were sages, all of us were experienced in the ways of the world, all knowledgeable in Torah, it would still be our responsibility to tell about the Exodus from Egypt. Whoever expands upon the story of the Exodus from Egypt is worthy of praise.

The Talmud's demand that we begin with the story of our degradation is meant to deepen our gratitude. We can appreciate freedom only when we remember what it was like not to be free, and when we consider how amazing it is that we are free. *Robert Goldenberg*

This is a good place for young children to pantomime. They can move around the table or into the living room and carry a very heavy bag of imaginary bricks on their backs as the backdrop to the singing of *Avadim Hayinu.*
Jeffrey Schein

עֲבָדִים הָיִינוּ עַתָּה בְּנֵי חוֹרִין

Avadim hayinu hayinu atah beney ḥorin beney ḥorin
Avadim hayinu atah atah beney ḥorin
Avadim hayinu atah atah beney ḥorin beney ḥorin.

The rabbinic sage Rav began with spiritual degradation:

מִתְּחִלָּה עוֹבְדֵי עֲבוֹדָה זָרָה הָיוּ אֲבוֹתֵינוּ. וְעַכְשָׁו קֵרְבָנוּ הַמָּקוֹם לַעֲבוֹדָתוֹ. שֶׁנֶּאֱמַר: וַיֹּאמֶר יְהוֹשֻׁעַ אֶל כָּל־הָעָם. כֹּה אָמַר יהוה אֱלֹהֵי יִשְׂרָאֵל. בְּעֵבֶר הַנָּהָר יָשְׁבוּ אֲבוֹתֵיכֶם מֵעוֹלָם, תֶּרַח אֲבִי אַבְרָהָם וַאֲבִי נָחוֹר. וַיַּעַבְדוּ אֱלֹהִים אֲחֵרִים. וָאֶקַּח אֶת־אֲבִיכֶם אֶת־אַבְרָהָם מֵעֵבֶר הַנָּהָר, וָאוֹלֵךְ אוֹתוֹ בְּכָל־אֶרֶץ כְּנָעַן. וָאַרְבֶּה אֶת־זַרְעוֹ, וָאֶתֶּן־לוֹ אֶת־יִצְחָק. וָאֶתֵּן לְיִצְחָק אֶת־יַעֲקֹב וְאֶת־עֵשָׂו... וְיַעֲקֹב וּבָנָיו יָרְדוּ מִצְרָיִם.

From the beginning, our ancestors worshiped idols. But now we have been brought near to God's service. As it is written, "Joshua said to the people: 'Thus said the Eternal One, the God of Israel: In olden times, your ancestors—Teraḥ, father of Abraham and Naḥor—lived beyond the Euphrates and worshiped other gods. But I took your father Abraham from beyond the Euphrates and led him through the whole land of Canaan and multiplied his offspring. I gave him Isaac, and to Isaac I gave Jacob and Esau . . . Jacob and his children went down to Egypt.'" *(Joshua 24:2–4)*

בָּרוּךְ הַמָּקוֹם
בָּרוּךְ הוּא.
בָּרוּךְ שֶׁנָּתַן תּוֹרָה לְעַמּוֹ יִשְׂרָאֵל
בָּרוּךְ הוּא.

Praised be the One who is in every place
Praised be the One.
Praised be the One who gave the Torah to the people Israel.
Praised be the One.

The two "beginnings" of the story speak of two different kinds of degradation—slavery and idol-worship. How are these related? Which is worse?
Robert Goldenberg

What is the slavery from which Israel escaped? Samuel argues that the escape is from physical slavery. Rav believes that it was idolatry and spiritual degradation that we escaped. It is hardly accidental that the Haggadah here gives both answers. There can never be complete spiritual freedom without physical freedom, and we cannot maintain physical freedom without spiritual discipline and clarity of mind. Thus we have not yet fully gone forth from Egypt when we have attained freedom. Our journey is complete only when we have a community that reinforces our ability to pursue justice and that acts out of concern for what has ultimate importance.
David Teutsch

Hamakom, a name of God, literally means "the place," implying the one who is everywhere. Why is this designation of God used? As wanderers, our ancestors came to realize that God is the ruler of the whole world, not only of the land of Israel.
Michael Strassfeld

THE FOUR CHILDREN

Four times the Torah speaks about children in connection with the telling of the Exodus story, but nothing is said about the character of these children. Rabbinic *midrash* viewed these passages not as simple repetitions but as representing different types of children.

There are four verses in the Torah that imply four types of children:

One who is wise
One who is wicked
One who is simple and
One who does not know enough to ask.

Yet we know that no child is all wise, all wicked, all simple, or incapable of asking anything. At different points in our lives, we have been all of these children:

One who is eager
One who is hostile
One who is passive and
One who is bewildered.

We have asked the cleverest of questions; we have challenged provocatively; we have simply wanted to know the answer; we have been so confused that we could not speak. We have been all of these children:

One who is aware
One who is alienated
One who is direct and
One who is silent.

In Exodus 6:6–7, God tells Moses to deliver this message to the Israelites: "I am YHWH, and I will **bring you out** *(vehotzeyti)* from under their forced labor, and I will **deliver you** *(vehitzalti)* from their bondage, and I will **redeem you** *(vega'alti)* with an outstretched arm and with great judgments, and I will **take you out** *(velakahti)* for a people." These four phrases can be understood as four stages of personal or political liberation: *vehotzeyti*—removing oneself physically from an oppressive situation; *vehitzalti*—dealing with internalized oppression, freeing the self; *vega'alti*—working with others to address the oppression and begin the process of redemption/liberation; and *velakahti*—realizing that one has been freed for something, and so working to envision and create a world where spiritual fulfillment and just community are possible. *Toba Spitzer*

Have you ever had a really great teacher, a teacher who loved your questions, whom you could always count on to at least try to answer you? It's really hard to be a wise child unless there are some wise grownups around to help you. *Joy Levitt*

Some seders, particularly those with several children between the ages of ten and seventeen, may benefit from a role reversal here. Ask participants to create the descriptions for the "four adults"—still named the *ḥaḥam*/wise, the *rashah*/ wicked, the *tam*/simple, and *she'eyno yodeya lishol*/ the one who does not know how to ask. *Jeffrey Schein*

Why do you think this illustration contains a bird's nest with four eggs wound into the fringes of the tallit? What do the four children and a tallit have in common? What could it mean that one child in the picture has more of the fringe inside, while other children may have it in their heads or not at all? Jeffrey Schrier

חָכָם מַה הוּא אוֹמֵר? מָה הָעֵדֹת וְהַחֻקִּים וְהַמִּשְׁפָּטִים
אֲשֶׁר צִוָּה יהוה אֱלֹהֵינוּ אוֹתָנוּ? וְאַף אַתָּה אֱמָר־לוֹ
כְּהִלְכוֹת הַפֶּסַח עַד: אֵין מַפְטִירִין בָּאֹכֶל אַחַר הָאֲפִיקוֹמָן.

What does the wise child ask? "What is the meaning of the decrees, laws, and rules that the Eternal One our God has commanded us?" *(Deuteronomy 6:20)*. You should tell this child all the laws of Pesaḥ down to the last detail, saying that nothing should be eaten after the *afi<u>k</u>oman*.

What does it mean to be a wise child? It means to be fully engaged in the community, to know the limits of your understanding, to be able to search for the answers to that which you do not know. At different points in our lives, we have been this child—inquisitive, caring, eager to learn and to understand, willing to ask for information we do not have, hopeful that an answer can be found.

רָשָׁע מַה הוּא אוֹמֵר? מָה הָעֲבֹדָה הַזֹּאת לָכֶם? לָכֶם וְלֹא
לוֹ. וּלְפִי שֶׁהוֹצִיא אֶת־עַצְמוֹ מִן הַכְּלָל כָּפַר בָּעִקָּר. וְאַף
אַתָּה הַקְהֵה אֶת־שִׁנָּיו וֶאֱמָר־לוֹ: בַּעֲבוּר זֶה עָשָׂה יהוה לִי
בְּצֵאתִי מִמִּצְרָיִם. לִי וְלֹא לוֹ. אִלּוּ הָיָה שָׁם, לֹא הָיָה נִגְאָל.

What does the wicked child ask? "What does this ritual mean to *you*?" *(Exodus 12:26)*. To you and not to this child. Since this child withdraws from the community and denies God's role in the Exodus, challenge the child by replying, "This is done because of what the Eternal One did for me when I went out of Egypt." *(Exodus 13:8)*. For me and not for you. Had you been there you would not have been redeemed.

What does it mean to be a wicked child? It means to stand apart from the community, to feel alienated and alone, depending only on yourself, to have little trust in the people around you to help you or answer your questions. At different points in our lives, we have been this child—detached, suspicious, challenging.

Why would this person not be redeemed? Could you imagine either God or Moses being so judgmental as to leave someone behind? What sin is so awful that it would cause one to deserve being left in Egypt?

No, the point is not that they would have abandoned the "wicked" child. This person who denies the community would have *refused* redemption! "What do you mean? Should *I* leave Egypt? How could they possibly mean *me* when they say 'Jew?' Or *Jude*. Or *Zhyd*." This refers to the Jews who denied their communal identity, or tried to hide themselves from reality. The World War I veteran who stayed in Germany until it was too late, sure that they would never harm a German hero. . . .

But it is not only freedom from political or religious repression that we refuse. Sometimes liberation from our own inner oppression is offered to us as a gift, and *still* we refuse to leave Egypt. *Arthur Green*

The wicked child is saying that we only have to think about Egypt; the rituals and *mitzvot* are unnecessary, since simply remembering the Exodus is enough. He does not understand that one must work for redemption and live in it afterwards, that intellectualizing is not enough.
Michael Strassfeld

In order to make a clear distinction between the wise and wicked child, some rabbinic versions changed the quoted biblical text. "What is the meaning . . . that the Eternal One our God has commanded *you*?" has been changed in the Jerusalem Talmud to "commanded *us*."
Michael Strassfeld

???

The tradition blames the wicked child because that child stands outside of the community. Do you agree? Why is it so bad to choose to stand apart? How should we respond to the "wicked" children among us? Should we give them space or shut them out? *Joy Levitt*

The wicked child might not be wicked at all; perhaps she is just expressing our doubts—what is the purpose of all this trouble you put yourself through at Pesaḥ? Are you really working for freedom? Annoyed at someone who gives voice to our own fears, we react harshly to hide our feelings. The wicked child becomes our scapegoat.
Michael Strassfeld

תָּם מַה הוּא אוֹמֵר? מַה זֹּאת? וְאָמַרְתָּ אֵלָיו: בְּחֹזֶק יָד הוֹצִיאָנוּ יהוה מִמִּצְרַיִם מִבֵּית עֲבָדִים.

What does the simple child ask? "What is this?" You shall say to that child, "It was with a mighty hand that the Eternal One brought us out of Egyptian bondage." *(Exodus 13:14)*

What does it mean to be a simple child? It means to see only one layer of meaning, to ask the most basic of questions, to be too innocent or impatient to grasp complicated questions. At different points in our lives, we have all been this child—simply curious and innocently unaware of the complexities around us.

וְשֶׁאֵינוֹ יוֹדֵעַ לִשְׁאוֹל, אַתְּ פְּתַח לוֹ. שֶׁנֶּאֱמַר: וְהִגַּדְתָּ לְבִנְךָ בַּיּוֹם הַהוּא לֵאמֹר, בַּעֲבוּר זֶה עָשָׂה יהוה לִי בְּצֵאתִי מִמִּצְרָיִם.

To the child who does not know enough to ask, you should begin as it is written, "You shall explain to your child on that day, 'It is because of what the Eternal One did for me when I went free from Egypt.'" *(Exodus 13:8)*

What does it mean to be a silent child? This can be the child of the wicked child, two generations removed from the Jewish community and no longer even able to criticize, only able to stand mute. It can be the passive child, who just shows up. Or it can be the child whose spiritual life is based on faith, not rational argument, the child who hears something deeper than words, who knows how to be silent and to listen to the surrounding silence.

We now begin to tell the story of the Exodus, which begins on page 52. Families with small children may want to turn to page 146 for the play. Others may wish to do the Bibliodrama, which is on page 151.

The wicked child is a skeptic interested only in asking questions, uninterested in any serious attempts to find answers. He is, then, a constantly doubting Jonah, waiting to be swallowed by his own questions.
Michael Strassfeld

The word *tam* has many connotations ranging from stupid, to simple, to innocent, to pious. How would you define this child? Is a person who asks a basic question stupid or just young or curious? Do you ever hold back from asking a question for fear that you ought to know the answer, that the question itself is too simple? In the Torah, Noah, Jacob, and Job are all called *tam*. Does this mean they were pious or simple? *Joy Levitt*

Sometimes we are silenced because we become convinced that we have nothing to contribute or that those we might address do not want to hear from us. Sometimes we are silenced because we believe that what we say will make no difference or even perhaps may make things worse. To come out of our silence, we need to recognize that people care about us and value who we are and what we can do. Each of us is sometimes silenced, and each of us can help end the silence of others. *David Teutsch*

When are you the silent child? When do you find that you can't speak, that words fail you, that you have nothing to say?
Joy Levitt

Because at different times in our lives we are wise and wicked, simple and silent, these four children represent the different aspects of our selves. We hear their voices and their questions as we tell the story of the Exodus.

אֲרַמִּי אֹבֵד אָבִי וַיֵּרֶד מִצְרַיְמָה, וַיָּגָר שָׁם בִּמְתֵי מְעָט. וַיְהִי־שָׁם לְגוֹי גָּדוֹל, עָצוּם וָרָב.

My father was a wandering Aramean. He went down to Egypt with meager numbers and sojourned there, but there he became a great and very populous nation. Deuteronomy 26:5

וְאֵלֶּה שְׁמוֹת בְּנֵי יִשְׂרָאֵל הַבָּאִים מִצְרָיְמָה אֵת יַעֲקֹב אִישׁ וּבֵיתוֹ בָּאוּ. רְאוּבֵן שִׁמְעוֹן לֵוִי וִיהוּדָה. יִשָּׂשכָר זְבוּלֻן וּבִנְיָמִן. דָּן וְנַפְתָּלִי גָּד וְאָשֵׁר. וַיְהִי כָּל־נֶפֶשׁ יֹצְאֵי יֶרֶךְ־יַעֲקֹב שִׁבְעִים נָפֶשׁ וְיוֹסֵף הָיָה בְמִצְרָיִם. וַיָּמָת יוֹסֵף וְכָל־אֶחָיו וְכֹל הַדּוֹר הַהוּא. וּבְנֵי יִשְׂרָאֵל פָּרוּ וַיִּשְׁרְצוּ וַיִּרְבּוּ וַיַּעַצְמוּ בִּמְאֹד מְאֹד וַתִּמָּלֵא הָאָרֶץ אֹתָם.

These are the names of the sons of Israel who came to Egypt with Jacob, each coming with his own household. Reuben, Simeon, Levi, and Judah; Issaḥar, Zebulun, and Benjamin; Dan and Naphtali, Gad and Asher. The total number of persons that were of Jacob's issue came to seventy, Joseph being already in Egypt. Joseph died, and all of his brothers, and all their generation. But the Israelites were fertile and prolific; they multiplied and increased very greatly, so that the land was filled with them. *Exodus 1:1–7*

The wise child asks, "Why does our story begin with the strange phrase, 'My father was a wandering Aramean'?"

The wicked child asks, "Why does it say that the sons of Jacob went *down* to the land of Mitzrayim, a place whose name can be related to the word *metzar,* or narrow place? Doesn't this mean that they freely chose not only a physical descent, but a spiritual one as well? And why did they stay when they could have left?"

The simple child asks, "What does it mean to be a great nation?"

The silent child wonders where this will all lead.

When the Israelites brought the fruits of their first harvest to the Temple in Jerusalem, they proclaimed the formula that began with the words, "My father was a wandering Aramean." It is recited not from the perspective of slaves, but of successful farmers in the Promised Land. Why was it important to recite this formula? "When you have eaten your fill and built fine houses to live in, and your herds and flocks have multiplied, and your silver and gold have increased, and everything you own has prospered, beware lest your heart grow haughty and you forget YHWH your God, who freed you from the land of Egypt, the house of slavery . . . and you say to yourselves. 'My own power and the might of my own hand have won this wealth for me'" (Deuteronomy 8:12–14; 17). As we celebrate our freedom and our bounty, we are reminded never to forget the many sources of our privilege, and the covenantal obligations that these privileges impose upon us. *Toba Spitzer*

To the wicked child: Would anyone freely choose to suffer? Wouldn't a choice that resulted in suffering come from a mind enslaved by confusion? Can we think about evil as ignorance, needing to learn? *Sylvia Boorstein*

To the wise child: The word Aramean is understood to refer to Jacob, much of whose life was spent in Aram. We begin the story with an awareness of our humble beginnings, for Jacob's wanderings mark him as a person with neither identity nor homeland. *Michael Strassfeld*

To the simple child: According to the rabbis, the Israelites became distinguished through the *mitzvot*. For they were not suspected of sexual immorality or of slander, and they did not change their names or language. What do you think sustained the Israelites in Egypt? What distinguishes and sustains a people today? *Mordechai Liebling*

וַיָּרֵעוּ אֹתָנוּ הַמִּצְרִים וַיְעַנּוּנוּ, וַיִּתְּנוּ עָלֵינוּ עֲבֹדָה קָשָׁה.

The Egyptians dealt harshly with us and oppressed us; they imposed heavy labor upon us. Deuteronomy 26:6

Bang, bang, bang,
hold your hammer low
Bang, bang, bang,
give a heavy blow
For it's work, work, work
every day and every night.
For it's work, work, work
when it's dark and when
it's light.

Oh listen, Oh listen,
Oh listen King Pharaoh
Oh listen, Oh listen,
please let my people go.
They want to go away,
they work too hard all day,
King Pharaoh, King Pharaoh,
what do you say?
No, no, no,
I will not let them go.

וַיָּקָם מֶלֶךְ־חָדָשׁ עַל־מִצְרָיִם אֲשֶׁר לֹא־יָדַע אֶת־יוֹסֵף.
וַיֹּאמֶר אֶל־עַמּוֹ הִנֵּה עַם בְּנֵי יִשְׂרָאֵל רַב וְעָצוּם מִמֶּנּוּ.
הָבָה נִתְחַכְּמָה לוֹ פֶּן־יִרְבֶּה וְהָיָה כִּי־תִקְרֶאנָה מִלְחָמָה
וְנוֹסַף גַּם־הוּא עַל־שֹׂנְאֵינוּ וְנִלְחַם־בָּנוּ וְעָלָה מִן־הָאָרֶץ.
וַיָּשִׂימוּ עָלָיו שָׂרֵי מִסִּים לְמַעַן עַנֹּתוֹ בְּסִבְלֹתָם. וְכַאֲשֶׁר
יְעַנּוּ אֹתוֹ כֵּן יִרְבֶּה וְכֵן יִפְרֹץ וַיָּקֻצוּ מִפְּנֵי בְּנֵי יִשְׂרָאֵל.
וַיְמָרְרוּ אֶת־חַיֵּיהֶם בַּעֲבֹדָה קָשָׁה בְּחֹמֶר וּבִלְבֵנִים
וּבְכָל־עֲבֹדָה בַּשָּׂדֶה בְּפָרֶךְ.

A new king arose over Egypt who did not know Joseph. And he said to his people, "Look, the Israelite people are much too numerous for us. Let us deal shrewdly with them, so that they do not increase; otherwise in the event of war they may join our enemies in fighting against us and rise from the ground." So they set taskmasters over them to oppress them with forced labor. But the more they were oppressed, the more they increased and spread out, so that the Egyptians came to dread the Israelites. Ruthlessly they made life bitter for them with harsh labor at mortar and bricks and with all sorts of tasks in the field. *Exodus 1:8–12; 14*

To the wicked child: Pharaoh requested, "Do me a favor and come work with me." Seeing Pharaoh working, the Israelites joined in and worked diligently all day long. At dusk, taskmasters appeared who counted the number of bricks each had made. Pharaoh said, "Now you must work to fulfill this same quota every day." Thus the slavery in Egypt has been likened to the taste of romaine lettuce *(maror)*—when fresh it tastes pleasant; later it becomes bitter. *Yalkut Shimoni 163*

To the simple child: The Egyptians would place a heavy burden on the weak and a light burden on the strong, the burden of the old on the young and of the young on the old. This was work without end and done for no purpose, for the Egyptians wanted not only to enslave them, but also to break their spirit. *Michael Strassfeld*

The wise child asks, "What do we learn from our suffering as strangers in Egypt?"

The wicked child asks, "How can the Israelites have let themselves be enslaved?"

The simple child asks, "What kind of hard labor did Pharaoh impose on the Israelites?"

The silent child is overwhelmed by the cry of the injured, the sigh of the weary, and the groans of those who are oppressed.

To the silent child: We can acknowledge that just as the suffering in the world is often beyond words, so also is the divine power of compassion. *Sylvia Boorstein*

To the wise child: The Torah teaches that our oppression must make us more sensitive to the oppression of others: "You shall not oppress a stranger, for you know the feelings of the stranger, having yourselves been strangers." *(Exodus 23:9)* *Joy Levitt*

To the skeptical child: What is unusual, even startling, about the story of the midwives is the fact that they are not punished by Pharaoh even when the nature of their rebellion is discovered. One would certainly have expected the ruler of Egypt to make an example of those who would thwart his decrees. Instead, Pharaoh resorts to a new strategy, charging the entire Egyptian population with the obligation to drown all male Israelite children at birth.

It seems Pharaoh either misses the point the midwives are making or chooses to ignore it. Nevertheless, in the act of the midwives we see the paradigm by which the freedom of the Israelites will ultimately be won. The Exodus will be effected through actions that defy the very authority of Pharaoh. *Richard Hirsh*

וַיֹּאמֶר מֶלֶךְ מִצְרַיִם לַמְיַלְּדֹת הָעִבְרִיֹּת אֲשֶׁר שֵׁם הָאַחַת
שִׁפְרָה וְשֵׁם הַשֵּׁנִית פּוּעָה. וַיֹּאמֶר בְּיַלֶּדְכֶן אֶת־הָעִבְרִיּוֹת
וּרְאִיתֶן עַל־הָאָבְנָיִם אִם־בֵּן הוּא וַהֲמִתֶּן אֹתוֹ וְאִם־בַּת
הִוא וָחָיָה. וַתִּירֶאןָ הַמְיַלְּדֹת אֶת־הָאֱלֹהִים וְלֹא עָשׂוּ
כַּאֲשֶׁר דִּבֶּר אֲלֵיהֶן מֶלֶךְ מִצְרָיִם וַתְּחַיֶּיןָ אֶת־הַיְלָדִים.
וַיִּקְרָא מֶלֶךְ־מִצְרַיִם לַמְיַלְּדֹת וַיֹּאמֶר לָהֶן מַדּוּעַ עֲשִׂיתֶן
הַדָּבָר הַזֶּה וַתְּחַיֶּיןָ אֶת־הַיְלָדִים. וַתֹּאמַרְןָ הַמְיַלְּדֹת
אֶל־פַּרְעֹה כִּי לֹא כַנָּשִׁים הַמִּצְרִיֹּת הָעִבְרִיֹּת כִּי־חָיוֹת
הֵנָּה בְּטֶרֶם תָּבוֹא אֲלֵהֶן הַמְיַלֶּדֶת וְיָלָדוּ. וַיֵּיטֶב אֱלֹהִים
לַמְיַלְּדֹת וַיִּרֶב הָעָם וַיַּעַצְמוּ מְאֹד. וַיְצַו פַּרְעֹה לְכָל־עַמּוֹ
לֵאמֹר כָּל־הַבֵּן הַיִּלּוֹד הַיְאֹרָה תַּשְׁלִיכֻהוּ וְכָל־הַבַּת תְּחַיּוּן.

The King of Egypt spoke to the Hebrew midwives, one of whom was named Shifrah and the other Puah, saying, "When you deliver the Hebrew women, look at the birth stool: if it is a boy, kill him; if it is a girl, let her live." The midwives, fearing God, did not do as the king of Egypt had told them; they let the boys live. So the king of Egypt summoned the midwives and said to them, "Why have you done this thing, letting the boys live?" The midwives said to Pharaoh, "Because the Hebrew women are not like the Egyptian women; they are vigorous. Before the midwife can come to them, they have given birth." And God dealt kindly with the midwives; and the people multiplied and increased greatly. Then Pharaoh charged all his people saying, "Every [Hebrew] boy that is born you shall throw into the Nile, but let every girl live." *Exodus 1:15–20; 22*

The thoughtful child asks, "What was it about these women that enabled them to defy authority?"

The skeptical child asks, "How come Pharaoh didn't kill the midwives?"

The direct child asks, "So who were the real heroes of the Exodus?"

The silent child sees that sometimes resistance is not only in word but in deed.

My grandson asked me, in response to some political event occurring at the time, whether I would ever lie under oath. I said that I would. Shifrah and Puah seem to have spoken words that were not factually true. Sometimes not speaking the truth is a higher moral cause. *Sylvia Boorstein*

To the direct child: When we think of going forth from Egypt, our attention is on the drama of the confrontation between Pharaoh and Moses and Aaron. But that conflict is only possible because of many less visible heroes. These include Shifrah and Puah as well as Miriam and Yo<u>h</u>eved (the mother of Moses), all of whom helped to make possible the victory achieved by Moses and Aaron. *David Teutsch*

וַנִּצְעַק אֶל־יהוה אֱלֹהֵי אֲבֹתֵינוּ וַיִּשְׁמַע יהוה אֶת־קֹלֵנוּ וַיַּרְא אֶת־עָנְיֵנוּ וְאֶת־עֲמָלֵנוּ
וְאֶת־לַחֲצֵנוּ.

We cried to the Eternal One, the God of our ancestors, who heard our plea and saw our plight, our misery, and our oppression. *Deuteronomy 26:7*

The event at the burning bush, the first revelation of God to Moses, is a key moment in the biblical narrative. Here the divine presence is entrusted to the human mind. All later revelations may be viewed as expansions or commentaries on this great gift, the verbalization of the Divine Selfhood in a single mysterious moment.

But what preparation was there leading up to this great event? The Bible seems to portray it as coming "out of nowhere." Not so the rabbis. They saw a Moses who was leader-in-training, caring for and loving each of the flock as he would later tend to the needs of all of his people. He led them "into the wilderness" ever in search of new pastures and fresh nourishment.

Jewish philosophers and mystics went still further, claiming that Moses' choice of the shepherd's life (over forty years!) was a search for *hitbodedut,* the state of being meditatively alone with God. Out in the wilderness, he was away from all distractions and could concentrate fully on the One. The revelation thus rewarded long years of practice and mental training. Inspiration, in other words, is nine-tenths preparation! *Arthur Green*

To save her child, Yoḥeved, an Israelite woman, placed him in a basket among the reeds by the bank of the Nile. His sister Miriam watched over him as he was discovered by the Pharaoh's daughter and raised in the palace. When he had grown up, he killed an Egyptian taskmaster who was beating an Israelite slave, and fled to Midian.

וּמֹשֶׁה הָיָה רֹעֶה אֶת־צֹאן יִתְרוֹ חֹתְנוֹ כֹּהֵן מִדְיָן וַיִּנְהַג
אֶת־הַצֹּאן אַחַר הַמִּדְבָּר וַיָּבֹא אֶל־הַר הָאֱלֹהִים חֹרֵבָה.
וַיֵּרָא מַלְאַךְ יהוה אֵלָיו בְּלַבַּת־אֵשׁ מִתּוֹךְ הַסְּנֶה וַיַּרְא וְהִנֵּה
הַסְּנֶה בֹּעֵר בָּאֵשׁ וְהַסְּנֶה אֵינֶנּוּ אֻכָּל. וַיֹּאמֶר מֹשֶׁה
אָסֻרָה־נָּא וְאֶרְאֶה אֶת־הַמַּרְאֶה הַגָּדֹל הַזֶּה מַדּוּעַ
לֹא־יִבְעַר הַסְּנֶה. וַיַּרְא יהוה כִּי סָר לִרְאוֹת וַיִּקְרָא אֵלָיו
אֱלֹהִים מִתּוֹךְ הַסְּנֶה וַיֹּאמֶר מֹשֶׁה מֹשֶׁה וַיֹּאמֶר הִנֵּנִי.
וַיֹּאמֶר אַל־תִּקְרַב הֲלֹם שַׁל־נְעָלֶיךָ מֵעַל רַגְלֶיךָ כִּי הַמָּקוֹם
אֲשֶׁר אַתָּה עוֹמֵד עָלָיו אַדְמַת־קֹדֶשׁ הוּא. וַיֹּאמֶר אָנֹכִי
אֱלֹהֵי אָבִיךָ אֱלֹהֵי אַבְרָהָם אֱלֹהֵי יִצְחָק וֵאלֹהֵי יַעֲקֹב.

Moses, tending the flock of his father-in-law Jethro, the priest of Midian, drove the flock into the wilderness and came to Ḥoreb, the mountain of God. An angel of the Eternal One appeared to him in a blazing fire out of a bush. He gazed, and there was a bush all aflame, yet the bush was not consumed. Moses said, "I must turn aside to look at this marvelous sight; why doesn't the bush burn up?" When the Eternal One saw that he had turned aside to look, God called to him out of the bush: "Moses! Moses!" He answered, "Here I am." And God said, "Do not come closer. Remove your sandals from your feet, for the place on which you stand is holy ground. I am the God of your father, the God of Abraham, the God of Isaac, and the God of Jacob." *Exodus 3:1–5*

To the silent child: Many parents can recall a time when, in response to the pain of one of their children (a colicky baby, a dyslexic third-grader, a confused adolescent), they had thought, "I wish I could have this pain instead of my child. I would gladly endure it knowing that they were suffering less."
Sylvia Boorstein

To the intellectual child: The "plight" refers to the enforced separation of husbands and wives. The Egyptians decreed that the men should sleep in the fields and the women in the cities in order to decrease their offspring. But the Israelite women would go to the fields and encourage their husbands by saying, "We shall not be enslaved forever; the Holy One will free us." Then they would come together and have children. Thus our ancestors were redeemed from Egypt due to the merit of the righteous women of that generation.
Exodus Rabbah 1:12

To the challenging child: The *midrash* tells us that to prevent any chance of rebellion, the Israelites were forbidden to complain about their lot, even to each other. However, under the pretense of mourning when Pharaoh died, they cried out their pain. *Michael Strassfeld*

וַיֹּאמֶר יהוה רָאֹה רָאִיתִי אֶת־עֳנִי עַמִּי אֲשֶׁר בְּמִצְרָיִם
וְאֶת־צַעֲקָתָם שָׁמַעְתִּי מִפְּנֵי נֹגְשָׂיו כִּי יָדַעְתִּי אֶת־מַכְאֹבָיו.
וָאֵרֵד לְהַצִּילוֹ מִיַּד מִצְרַיִם וּלְהַעֲלֹתוֹ מִן־הָאָרֶץ הַהִוא
אֶל־אֶרֶץ טוֹבָה וּרְחָבָה אֶל־אֶרֶץ זָבַת חָלָב וּדְבָשׁ. וְעַתָּה
לְכָה וְאֶשְׁלָחֲךָ אֶל־פַּרְעֹה וְהוֹצֵא אֶת־עַמִּי בְנֵי־יִשְׂרָאֵל
מִמִּצְרָיִם.

And the Eternal One continued, "I have marked well the plight of my people in Egypt and have heeded their outcry because of their taskmasters; yes, I am mindful of their sufferings. I have come down to rescue them from the Egyptians and to bring them out of that land to a good and spacious land flowing with milk and honey. Come, therefore, I will send you to Pharaoh, and you shall free My people, the Israelites, from Egypt." *Exodus 3:7–8, 10*

The intellectual child asks, "What is the full meaning of the expression: 'God saw the plight . . .'?"

The challenging child asks, "Why did the Israelites wait so long before they cried out to God?"

The direct child asks, "Why did God finally hear the plea of the Israelites?"

The silent child wonders whether God suffers when we suffer.

The Torah records the unique and indispensable role of Moses in the drama of redemption and the forging of the Israelites into a nation. Later, the rabbis minimized the role of Moses in the traditional Haggadah because they feared that belief in a human savior might displace faith in the God of salvation. Today we understand that it is not an issue of God *or* people, but of God working *through* people, as we become agents of the godliness that makes for freedom.
Richard Hirsh

Moses created a people but the Jewish people also created Moses. The portrait of Moses has grown out of Jewish experience; we cannot know to what extent the historical Moses and the leader we admire are in fact one. What is important is that the Jewish people conceived of such a one to be their hero, their primary prophet and teacher. In so doing, we committed ourselves to a life of freedom, a life incapable of reconciliation with oppression, tyranny, and enslavement.
Ira Eisenstein

וַיּוֹצִאֵנוּ יהוה מִמִּצְרַיִם בְּיָד חֲזָקָה וּבִזְרֹעַ נְטוּיָה וּבְמֹרָא גָּדֹל וּבְאֹתוֹת וּבְמֹפְתִים.

Then the Eternal One freed us from Egypt by a mighty hand, by an outstretched arm and awesome power, and by signs and portents. *Deuteronomy 26:8*

וַיֹּאמֶר יהוה אֶל מֹשֶׁה אַתָּה תְדַבֵּר אֵת כָּל־אֲשֶׁר אֲצַוֶּךָּ
וְאַהֲרֹן אָחִיךָ יְדַבֵּר אֶל־פַּרְעֹה וְשִׁלַּח אֶת־בְּנֵי־יִשְׂרָאֵל
מֵאַרְצוֹ. וַאֲנִי אַקְשֶׁה אֶת־לֵב פַּרְעֹה וְהִרְבֵּיתִי אֶת־אֹתֹתַי
וְאֶת־מוֹפְתַי בְּאֶרֶץ מִצְרָיִם.

The Eternal One replied to Moses, "You shall repeat all that I command you, and your brother Aaron shall speak to Pharaoh to let the Israelites depart from his land. But I will harden Pharaoh's heart, that I may multiply my signs and marvels in the land of Egypt." *Exodus 7:1b–3*

To the simple child: Certainly God could have given the Israelites the means for self-defense. But some say God preferred not to sanction the use of the fists. While at that moment they might merely have defended themselves against evildoers, by such means the way of the fist spreads through the world and defenders become aggressors.
Rabbi Aaron of Tamaret, translated by Everett Gendler

The Torah wraps the story of Pesaḥ in a myriad of miracles: the ten plagues, the parting of the sea, the mannah of the desert . . . all impressive, but difficult for moderns to accept. Yet even the Torah understood that the essence of the Exodus was not the supernatural synopsis but the fundamental value of liberation. Miracles dazzle but are quickly deciphered; they may be spellbinding but they are not sustaining. One of the true miracles of history has been the ability of the Jewish people throughout the generations to sustain a faith in freedom and in the God that stands for freedom. *Richard Hirsh*

The aware child asks, "Why was the Eternal One performing all the signs and marvels?"

The challenging child asks, "Whose fault was it that Pharaoh kept preventing the Israelites from leaving? You keep saying that God stiffened Pharaoh's heart. What happened to free will? How can you blame Pharaoh if God wouldn't even let him make up his own mind?"

The simple child asks, "How could God do such a thing?"

The confused child does not know how to ask the deepest question, "Did it really have to be this way?"

To the challenging child: There have always been people of power whose inclination to evil renders them undeserving of forgiveness or compassion. No matter how we twist the text, we cannot avoid the uncomfortable conclusion that for some actions there can be no repentance. Certain behaviors seem impervious to treatment.

This was not the first or last time in history that innocent people paid a price for the decisions of the powerful who controlled the machinery of politics and war. God, the power that makes for freedom, cannot penetrate all hearts that remain blind to injustice, deaf to pain, and speechless in the presence of suffering.
Richard Hirsh

שָׁלַח חֹשֶׁךְ וַיַּחְשִׁךְ וְלֹא מָרוּ אֶת־דְּבָרוֹ. הָפַךְ אֶת־מֵימֵיהֶם
לְדָם וַיָּמֶת אֶת־דְּגָתָם. שָׁרַץ אַרְצָם צְפַרְדְּעִים בְּחַדְרֵי
מַלְכֵיהֶם. אָמַר וַיָּבֹא עָרֹב כִּנִּים בְּכָל־גְּבוּלָם. נָתַן גִּשְׁמֵיהֶם
בָּרָד אֵשׁ לֶהָבוֹת בְּאַרְצָם. וַיַּךְ גַּפְנָם וּתְאֵנָתָם וַיְשַׁבֵּר עֵץ
גְּבוּלָם. אָמַר וַיָּבֹא אַרְבֶּה וְיֶלֶק וְאֵין מִסְפָּר. וַיֹּאכַל
כָּל־עֵשֶׂב בְּאַרְצָם וַיֹּאכַל פְּרִי אַדְמָתָם. וַיַּךְ כָּל־בְּכוֹר
בְּאַרְצָם רֵאשִׁית לְכָל־אוֹנָם.

God sent darkness; it was very dark;
did they not defy God's word?
God turned their waters into blood
and killed their fish.
Their land teemed with frogs,
even the rooms of their king.
Swarms of insects came at God's command,
lice, throughout their country.
God gave them hail for rain,
and flaming fire in their land.
God struck their vines and fig trees,
broke down the trees of their country.
Locusts came at God's command,
grasshoppers without number.
They devoured every green thing in the land;
they consumed the produce of the soil.
God struck down every first-born in the land,
the first fruit of their vigor. *Psalm 105:28–36*

Psalm 105 is another biblical version of the plagues. Compare the order of the plagues to the order listed on page 61. Is it the same or different? Which of the ten plagues are missing from this psalm?
Michael Strassfeld

One morning when Pharaoh
awoke in his bed
There were frogs on his head
and frogs in his bed
Frogs on his nose and frogs on
his toes
Frogs here, frogs there, frogs
were jumping everywhere.

This comment of the wise child, a reference to a *midrash* about God's rebuke to the angels, is a profound challenge to us as modern Jews. In what ways does our liberation come at the expense of others, and in what ways can we alleviate any injustice done? At whose expense have we as a community achieved a remarkable level of economic prosperity? How do we acknowledge the suffering, inadvertent or otherwise, caused to others by the establishment of the State of Israel? How can each of us, as individuals, come into our full selves without diminishing the selfhood of others? *Toba Spitzer*

As each plague is mentioned, take a drop of wine from the cup and recite:

דָּם, צְפַרְדֵּעַ, כִּנִּים, עָרוֹב, דֶּבֶר, שְׁחִין, בָּרָד, אַרְבֶּה, חֹשֶׁךְ,
מַכַּת בְּכוֹרוֹת

Dam, Tzefarde'a, Kinim, Arov, Dever, Shehin, Barad, Arbeh, Hoshe, Makat Behorot

The Holy One brought ten plagues upon the Egyptians, and they were:
Blood, Frogs, Lice, Beasts, Cattle Plague, Boils, Hail, Locusts, Darkness, Death of the Firstborn

---

The wise child says, "We spill the wine from our cup because our salvation came at the expense of the suffering of others. At the crossing of the sea, the ministering angels wanted to sing praises to God. But God silenced them, saying, 'My children are drowning in the sea and you want to sing before me?'"

The vengeful child says, "We spill the wine from the cup because *our* blood has been spilled. There was a dispute in heaven about how much mercy God should show the Egyptians, until the angel Gabriel showed God a brick from Egypt with a baby entombed in it. 'Master of the world,' he said, 'thus did they enslave the Israelites.' God immediately sentenced the Egyptians and drowned them in the sea."

The innocent child says, "We spill the wine from the cup because our blood was spilled and their blood was spilled. We are all diminished when blood is shed."

The unaware child enjoys spilling the drops.

How can we understand God's role in the death of the first born? One explanation suggests that all who did not defend the Israelite slaves in Egypt are responsible for what Pharaoh imposed. Thus, God's punishment of the Egyptians was justified. Another explanation holds that only in hindsight did the Israelites see the hand of God in the death of the Egyptians. God does not intervene in human history this way. Salvation is defined in the human mind. By this reckoning, what is important is not whether the firstborn died, but whether we can see the power of human redemption in our lives as flowing from the divine. How do we assume the role of redeemers in a world where confronting tyranny is so difficult? *David Teutsch*

If we only pour ten drops of wine from our cups and do nothing more, we do not understand the significance of the act. Our joy cannot be complete when there is harshness, cruelty, or suffering in the world. We cannot wait for others to tackle the injustices of our time. What will you do this year? *David Teutsch*

וַיֻּגַּד לְמֶלֶךְ מִצְרַיִם כִּי בָרַח הָעָם, וַיֵּהָפֵךְ לְבַב פַּרְעֹה
וַעֲבָדָיו אֶל הָעָם וַיֹּאמְרוּ מַה זֹּאת עָשִׂינוּ כִּי שִׁלַּחְנוּ
אֶת־יִשְׂרָאֵל מֵעָבְדֵנוּ. וַיִּרְדְּפוּ מִצְרַיִם אַחֲרֵיהֶם וַיַּשִּׂיגוּ
אוֹתָם. וַיָּבֹאוּ בְנֵי יִשְׂרָאֵל בְּתוֹךְ הַיָּם בַּיַּבָּשָׁה, וְהַמַּיִם לָהֶם
חֹמָה מִימִינָם וּמִשְּׂמֹאלָם. וַיִּרְדְּפוּ מִצְרַיִם וַיָּבֹאוּ אַחֲרֵיהֶם,
כֹּל סוּס פַּרְעֹה רִכְבּוֹ וּפָרָשָׁיו אֶל תּוֹךְ הַיָּם. וַיָּשֻׁבוּ הַמַּיִם
וַיְכַסּוּ אֶת־הָרֶכֶב וְאֶת־הַפָּרָשִׁים לְכֹל חֵיל פַּרְעֹה הַבָּאִים
אַחֲרֵיהֶם בַּיָּם, לֹא נִשְׁאַר בָּהֶם עַד אֶחָד.

When the King of Egypt was told that the people had fled, Pharaoh and his courtiers had a change of heart about the people and said, "What is this we have done, releasing Israel from our service?" As the Israelites were departing defiantly, the Egyptians gave chase to them and overtook them.

The Israelites went into the sea on dry ground, the waters forming a wall for them on their right and on their left. The Egyptians came in pursuit after them into the sea, all of Pharaoh's horses, chariots, and horsemen. The waters turned back and covered the chariots and the horsemen—Pharaoh's entire army that followed them into the sea; not one of them remained. *Exodus 14:5, 8b–9; 22–23; 28*

Finally, Pharaoh and his courtiers had made the right decision, getting rid of this oppressed and angry populace whose presence had brought them so much grief. But they were unable to let this decision stand! They were afraid the Israelites had made fools of them and would now perhaps join their other enemies to turn against them. One would think that ten plagues would have been enough *intifada* for those foolish Egyptians. But some people never seem to learn.
Arthur Green

When you are about to leave Egypt—any Egypt—do not stop to think, "But how will I earn a living out there?" One who stops to "make provisions for the way" will never get out of Egypt.
Rabbi Naḥman of Bratzlav

Some scholars suggest that Miriam was the author of the entire Song at the Sea, not just this single verse. In the process of elevating Moses, the editors of the text attributed the whole song to him. But the tradition of Miriam was so strong among the people that it could not be suppressed. A remnant of her voice remains with us.

When we sing her song, we remember Miriam, who encouraged her people to sing and to dance on their way to freedom. We think of our own journey into uncharted landscapes, and of the song inside each of us waiting to be sung. Like Miriam, without knowing the steps, we take a chance and dance.
Sandy Eisenberg Sasso

LET MY PEOPLE GO

When Israel was in Egypt Land,
  Let my people go.
Oppressed so hard they could not stand,
  Let my people go.

(Chorus)
Go down, Moses, way down in Egypt Land,
Tell ol' Pharaoh
  Let my people go.

Thus said the Lord, bold Moses said,
  Let my people go.
If not I'll smite your first-born dead.
  Let my people go.
(Chorus)

As Israel stood by the waterside,
  Let my people go.
By God's command it did divide,
  Let my people go.
(Chorus)

Lift Miriam's Cup and recite:

וַתִּקַּח מִרְיָם הַנְּבִיאָה אֲחוֹת אַהֲרֹן אֶת־הַתֹּף בְּיָדָהּ, וַתֵּצֶאןָ כָל־הַנָּשִׁים אַחֲרֶיהָ בְּתֻפִּים וּבִמְחֹלֹת. וַתַּעַן לָהֶם מִרְיָם: שִׁירוּ לַיהוה כִּי גָאֹה גָּאָה, סוּס וְרֹכְבוֹ רָמָה בַיָּם.

Then Miriam, the prophetess, Aaron's sister, took a timbrel in her hand, and all the women went after her in dance with timbrels. And Miriam chanted for them: Sing to The Eternal One, for God has triumphed gloriously; horse and driver God has hurled into the sea. *Exodus 15:20–21*

Set the cup down.

We meet Miriam here again at the crossing of the Sea, leading the women in dance with timbrels. I remember the moment in my childhood when that line struck me with surprise. I wasn't surprised that she led the women in celebration. That seemed natural. But how often had we been told that they had left Egypt in extreme haste, with no time even to let their dough rise? It seemed so strange that women who were so busy rushing around they could hardly pack food would find time to pack their timbrels!

We can only imagine that these timbrels had the status of religious ceremonial objects. Today we might remember to take candlesticks. Back then, a good Jewish girl made sure she had her drum. *Lori Lefkovitz*

Choose one of the following songs.

MIRIAM'S SONG

(Chorus)
And the women dancing with their timbrels
Followed Miriam as she sang her song.
Sing a song to the One whom we've exalted.
Miriam and the women danced and danced the whole
night long.

And Miriam was a weaver of unique variety.
The tapestry she wove was one which sang our history.
With every thread and every strand she crafted her
delight.
A woman touched with spirit, she dances to the light.
(Chorus)

As Miriam stood upon the shores and gazed across the
sea,
The wonder of this miracle she soon came to believe.
Whoever thought the sea would part with an outstretched
hand,
And we would pass to freedom, and march to the
promised land.
(Chorus)

And Miriam the Prophet took her timbrel in her hand,
And all the women followed her just as she had planned.
And Miriam raised her voice with song.
She sang with praise and might,
We've just lived through a miracle, we're going to dance
tonight.

Debbie Friedman

Birth is a defining moment, and the passage through the Sea of Reeds, as the birthing of the Jewish people, is a moment awaiting articulation. Our first act as a people, as a community . . . is to sing! Not to pray, not to enact law, not to organize . . . but to sing!
Richard Hirsh

Modern Bible scholars maintain that the Israelites crossed not the Red Sea *(Yam Suf)* but the Reed Sea *(Yam Sif)*. If so, they crossed an area that is sometimes dry and sometimes flooded. This would make the miracle one of timing rather than of suspension of the laws of nature.

The way the event happened is not as important as the fact that it happened, or at least that it is remembered this way by the Jewish people. Regardless of the risks, the Israelites had to have the courage to cross. We cannot afford to miss any opportunity for redemption.
David Teutsch

MIRIAM BY THE SHORES

By the shores, by the shores,
Of the Red, Red Sea
By the shores of the Red, Red Sea;
The light of day lit up the night
The children, they were free.
(Chorus)
And Miriam took her timbrel out and all the
women/people danced (2)
Vatikaḥ Miriam hanevi'ah et hatof beyadah, vateytzena
kol hanashim aḥareha.

They danced so hard, they danced so fast;
They danced with movement strong
Laughed and cried, brought out alive
They danced until the dawn.
Some carrying child, some baking bread
Weeping as they prayed
But when they heard the music start
They put their pain away
(Chorus)
Enticed to sing, drawn to move
Mesmerized by such emotion
The men saw us reach out our hands
Stretching across the ocean.

As they watched, and they clapped, they began to sway
Drawn to ride the wave
and all our brothers began to dance
They dance with us today!

They danced, we dance
Sheḥina dances
They danced the night away
And all the people began to sing
We're singing 'til this day!
(Chorus)

Rayzel Raphael

I SHALL SING TO THE LORD A NEW SONG

I, Miriam, stand at the sea
and turn
to face the desert
stretching endless and
still.
My eyes are dazzled
The sky brilliant blue
Sunburnt sands unyielding white.
My hands turn to dove wings.
My arms
reach
for the sky
and I want to sing
the song rising inside me.
My mouth open
I stop.
Where are the words?
Where is the melody?
In a moment of panic
My eyes go blind.
Can I take a step
Without knowing a
Destination?
Will I falter
Will I fall
Will the ground sink away from under me?
The song still unformed—
How can I sing?

To take the first step—
To sing a new song—
Is to close one's eyes and dive
into unknown waters.
For a moment knowing nothing risking all—
But then to discover

The waters are friendly
The ground is firm.
And the song—
the song rises again.
Out of my mouth
come words lifting the wind.
And I hear
for the first
the song
that has been in my heart
silent
unknown
even to me.

Ruth Sohn

The border for this illustration comes from a piece of cloth woven by Ethiopian Jewish women after their rescue to Israel. What elements of the poem can be found in the illustration? Jeffrey Schrier

MEDITERRANEAN OR GREAT SEA
EGYPT
ARABIA PETRAEA
WILDERNESS
Portion of route known
conjectural
The
PENINSULA OF Mt SINAI.
A MAP TO ILUSTRATE THE
Wanderings of the Israelites
From Egypt to Canaan.
L.U. SNEAD-PUBLISHER
WELLSVILLE, N.Y.
The
PENINSULA OF Mt SINAI.
A MAP TO ILUSTRATE THE
Wanderings of the Israelites
From Egypt to Canaan.

DAYENU

דינו

אִלּוּ הוֹצִיאָנוּ מִמִּצְרַיִם,
וְלֹא עָשָׂה בָהֶם שְׁפָטִים, דַּיֵּנוּ:
אִלּוּ עָשָׂה בָהֶם שְׁפָטִים,
וְלֹא קָרַע לָנוּ אֶת־הַיָּם, דַּיֵּנוּ:
אִלּוּ קָרַע לָנוּ אֶת־הַיָּם,
וְלֹא הֶעֱבִירָנוּ בְתוֹכוֹ בֶּחָרָבָה, דַּיֵּנוּ:
אִלּוּ הֶעֱבִירָנוּ בְתוֹכוֹ בֶּחָרָבָה,
וְלֹא סִפֵּק צָרְכֵּנוּ בַּמִּדְבָּר אַרְבָּעִים שָׁנָה, דַּיֵּנוּ:
אִלּוּ סִפֵּק צָרְכֵּנוּ בַּמִּדְבָּר אַרְבָּעִים שָׁנָה,
וְלֹא הֶאֱכִילָנוּ אֶת־הַמָּן, דַּיֵּנוּ:
אִלּוּ הֶאֱכִילָנוּ אֶת־הַמָּן,
וְלֹא נָתַן לָנוּ אֶת־הַשַּׁבָּת, דַּיֵּנוּ:
אִלּוּ נָתַן לָנוּ אֶת־הַשַּׁבָּת,
וְלֹא קֵרְבָנוּ לִפְנֵי הַר סִינַי, דַּיֵּנוּ:
אִלּוּ קֵרְבָנוּ לִפְנֵי הַר סִינַי,
וְלֹא נָתַן לָנוּ אֶת־הַתּוֹרָה, דַּיֵּנוּ:
אִלּוּ נָתַן לָנוּ אֶת־הַתּוֹרָה,
וְלֹא הִכְנִיסָנוּ לְאֶרֶץ יִשְׂרָאֵל, דַּיֵּנוּ:
אִלּוּ הִכְנִיסָנוּ לְאֶרֶץ יִשְׂרָאֵל,
וְלֹא בָנָה לָנוּ אֶת־בֵּית הַבְּחִירָה, דַּיֵּנוּ:

Ilu hotzi hotzianu hotzianu mimitzrayim
hotzianu mimitzrayim dayenu
Day, dayenu (3) dayenu dayenu
Ilu natan natan lanu natan lanu et hashabbat
natan lanu et hashabbat dayenu
Day, dayenu (3) dayenu dayenu
Ilu natan natan lanu natan lanu et hatorah
natan lanu et hatorah dayenu

In what sense is each moment of liberation enough? *Dayenu* signifies deep acceptance and gratitude. We acknowledge the present moment. In the affirmation of *dayenu,* we are fully present to the preciousness of each act of redemption and care—dividing the sea, leading us across, caring for us in the desert. . . . We receive each moment with love. This acceptance allows us to move to the next moment and receive the waiting gift. When we greet each moment with conditions, judgments, and expectations—"well, this really isn't quite where we need to be" or "wait a second, this is not what we were promised" or "hey, what's coming next?"—our expectations keep us tense. We are not free. We are not available to receive the next moment. Our fantasies about the past and our desire to control the future cut us off from the wonders of this moment. They shut us in a prison of disappointment and suffering. *Dayenu* is a great liberator. It is a jolt into the presence of awe, compassion, attention, and freedom.
Sheila Peltz Weinberg

The verse that proclaims that it would have been enough had God helped us reach Mount Sinai without giving us the Torah makes no sense according to Rabbi Levi Yitzhak of Berdichev. What would have been the purpose of coming to Sinai if there was to be no Torah, no revelation?

The answer, he says, lies in what happened to Israel in the three days of preparation for the great event. Each one present, he says (and of course all of us were present at Sinai), sincerely and deeply opened his/her heart to Torah, casting aside all material concerns in order to hear God's word. Then we were all able to discover the entire Torah already implanted within our own hearts. Each of us contains Torah within us; it is only our enslavement to externals that keeps us from turning inward to find it. The *promise* of revelation was enough, he says, to evoke this discovery/revelation from within. *Arthur Green*

In what ways do the maps of the Sinai in this illustration complement Dayenu*? Could* Dayenu *be telling us that, as important as the destination is, so too is the awesome process of the journey itself?*
Jeffrey Schrier

Liberation comes in small steps. Dayenu teaches us not to despair when the ultimate end seems far away. We have to fully acknowledge and appreciate each struggle that we win, each step towards freedom that we take, if we are to have the strength and conviction to continue. *Toba Spitzer*

Had God taken us out of Egypt but had not . . .
divided the sea for us—dayenu. . . .
Had God given us Shabbat but had not enabled us to reach Mount Sinai—dayenu.
Had God enabled us to reach Mount Sinai but had not given us the Torah—dayenu.
Had God given us the Torah but had not brought us into the Land of Israel—it would have been enough—dayenu.

In what sense would it have been "enough" to be led out of Egypt and then stranded in the desert? This all-too-familiar song suggests that even when our liberation remains incomplete we must still acknowledge the blessings we enjoy, and we must still take care to use them properly. When the people wandering in the desert forgot *dayenu*, they lost what blessings they had. *Robert Goldenberg*

בְּכָל־דּוֹר וָדוֹר חַיָּב אָדָם לִרְאוֹת אֶת־עַצְמוֹ כְּאִלּוּ הוּא יָצָא מִמִּצְרָֽיִם, שֶׁנֶּאֱמַר: וְהִגַּדְתָּ לְבִנְךָ בַּיּוֹם הַהוּא לֵאמֹר: בַּעֲבוּר זֶה עָשָׂה יהוה לִי בְּצֵאתִי מִמִּצְרָֽיִם. לֹא אֶת־אֲבוֹתֵֽינוּ בִּלְבָד גָּאַל הַקָּדוֹשׁ בָּרוּךְ הוּא, אֶלָּא אַף אוֹתָֽנוּ גָּאַל עִמָּהֶם. שֶׁנֶּאֱמַר: וְאוֹתָֽנוּ הוֹצִיא מִשָּׁם לְמַֽעַן הָבִיא אֹתָֽנוּ לָתֶת לָֽנוּ אֶת־הָאָֽרֶץ אֲשֶׁר נִשְׁבַּע לַאֲבֹתֵֽינוּ.

In every generation, each individual should feel personally redeemed from Egypt, as it is said: "You shall explain to your child on that day, it is because of what the Eternal One did for me when I went free from Egypt." *(Exodus 13:8)*. For God redeemed not only our ancestors; God redeemed us with them, as it is said, "God freed us from there, that God might take us and give us the land that God had promised on oath to our ancestors." *Deuteronomy 6:23*

This paragraph—"In every generation"—is the heart of the seder, and, to my mind, the heart of Judaism. We are commanded to find ourselves within this story and to make this story our own. Slavery happened to each of us; redemption happened to each of us. The message of hope at the core of the story—the reality of the possibility of liberation in the midst of slavery—is the gift we bring to a world broken by the continual oppressions that human beings inflict upon one another.

It is from this awareness of the possibility of transformation that we come to the next point of the seder, to singing a "new song" before God. By weaving our own stories of oppression and liberation into this master story, each of us renews the message of hope in our own generation. By realizing our place in the ancient story, we are moved to sing a "new song," a new way of understanding slavery and freedom, and of what it means to exalt the One. *Toba Spitzer*

Lift the cup.

לְפִיכָךְ אֲנַֽחְנוּ חַיָּבִים לְהוֹדוֹת לְהַלֵּל לְשַׁבֵּֽחַ לְפָאֵר לְרוֹמֵם לְהַדֵּר לְבָרֵךְ לְעַלֵּה וּלְקַלֵּס לְמִי שֶׁעָשָׂה לַאֲבוֹתֵֽינוּ וְלָֽנוּ אֶת־כָּל־הַנִּסִּים הָאֵֽלּוּ. הוֹצִיאָֽנוּ מֵעַבְדוּת לְחֵרוּת מִיָּגוֹן לְשִׂמְחָה מֵאֵֽבֶל לְיוֹם טוֹב וּמֵאֲפֵלָה לְאוֹר גָּדוֹל וּמִשִּׁעְבּוּד לִגְאֻלָּה וְנֹאמַר לְפָנָיו שִׁירָה חֲדָשָׁה, הַלְלוּיָהּ.

Therefore we should revere, adore, glorify, and praise the One who performed all these miracles for our ancestors and for us. God took us from slavery to freedom, from sorrow to happiness, from mourning to celebration, from darkness to great light, from slavery to redemption.

We sing before God a new song. Halleluyah.

Set the cup down.

Venomar lifanav shirah ḥadashah (2)
Halleluyah (4)

לְפִיכָךְ אֲנַחְנוּ חַיָּבִים לַעֲבוֹד לִצְעֹק לְהִשְׁתַּדֵּל לְהִלָּחֵם בְּעַד גְּאוּלַּת כֹּל יוֹשְׁבֵי תֵּבֵל כְּמוֹ שֶׁנֶּאֱמַר: וְגֵר לֹא תִלְחָץ וְאַתֶּם יְדַעְתֶּם אֶת־נֶפֶשׁ הַגֵּר כִּי־גֵרִים הֱיִיתֶם בְּאֶרֶץ מִצְרָיִם. וּלְתַקֵּן עוֹלָם בְּמַלְכוּת שַׁדַּי וְכֹל בְּנֵי בָשָׂר יִקְרְאוּ בְּשִׁמְךָ כְּמוֹ שֶׁנֶּאֱמַר: הִנֵּה יָמִים בָּאִים נְאֻם אֲדֹנָי יהוה וְהִשְׁלַחְתִּי רָעָב בָּאָרֶץ לֹא־רָעָב לַלֶּחֶם וְלֹא־צָמָא לַמַּיִם כִּי אִם־לִשְׁמֹעַ אֵת דִּבְרֵי יהוה. וְיִגַּל כַּמַּיִם מִשְׁפָּט וּצְדָקָה כְּנַחַל אֵיתָן. אָז נָשִׁיר שִׁיר חָדָשׁ: לֹא יִשָּׂא גוֹי אֶל גּוֹי חֶרֶב וְלֹא יִלְמְדוּ עוֹד מִלְחָמָה. וְנֹאמַר הַלְלוּיָה.

Therefore we should work, speak out, strive, and fight for the redemption of all the peoples of the world, as it is written: "You shall not oppress a stranger, for you know the feelings of the stranger, having yourselves been strangers in the land of Egypt" *(Exodus 23:9)*. Then the power of your rule will repair the world, and all the creatures of flesh will call on your name, as it is written: "A time is coming—declares my Eternal God—when I will send a famine upon the land: not a hunger for bread or a thirst for water, but for hearing the words of the Eternal One." "So let justice well up like water, righteousness like an unfailing stream" *(Amos 8:11, 5:24)*. Then we will sing a new song:

"Nation shall not lift up sword against nation. Let them learn no longer ways of war" (*Isaiah 2:4)*. And let us say Halleluyah.

Lo yisa goy el goy herev lo yilmedu od milḥamah.

Now is the time to make justice a reality for all of God's children. . . . [And] we will not be satisfied until justice rolls down like water and righteousness like a mighty stream. . . .

I say to you today, my friends, even though we face the difficulties of today and tomorrow, I still have a dream. It is a dream deeply rooted in the American dream. I have a dream that one day this nation will rise up and live out the true meaning of its creed: "We hold these truths to be self-evident, that all men are created equal. . . ." This is our hope.

With this faith we will be able to hew out of the mountain of despair a stone of hope. With this faith we will be able to transform the jangling discords of our nation into a beautiful symphony of brotherhood. With this faith we will be able to work together, to pray together, to struggle together, to go to jail together, to stand up for freedom together, knowing that we will be free one day. . . .

So let freedom ring from the prodigious hilltops of New Hampshire. Let freedom ring from the mighty mountains of New York. Let freedom ring from the heightening Alleghenies of Pennsylvania. Let freedom ring from the snowcapped Rockies of Colorado. Let freedom ring from Stone Mountain of Georgia; let freedom ring from Lookout Mountain of Tennessee; let freedom ring from every hill and molehill of Mississippi—from every mountainside, let freedom ring.

And when this happens, when we allow freedom to ring, when we let it ring from every village, from every hamlet, from every state and every city, we will be able to speed up that day when all of God's children, black and white, Jew and Gentile, Protestant and Catholic, will be able to join hands and sing in the words of the old Negro spiritual: "Free at last! Free at last! Thank God almighty, we are free at last!"

Martin Luther King, Jr.

Why start *Hallel* before dinner? It alerts us to the fact that the celebration begins here with rejoicing about *Pesaḥ Mitzrayim,* the first Pesaḥ in Egypt, and that first redemption. But the rejoicing does not end here. It continues through the meal, which marks the present. The meal represents another form of redemption, for this food not only sustains life but gives us the opportunity to celebrate it. And then Hallel continues after the Grace after Meals. It extends to the part of the seder where *Pesaḥ le'atid*—the Pesaḥ of the future—is discussed. We leave a bit of the celebration for the future in the hope that we will live to see a world fully redeemed. *David Teutsch*

The following Psalms, along with those recited after the meal, are known as Hallel/*Psalms of Praise. Customarily recited at festival morning services, they are traditionally part of the seder celebration.*

הַלְלוּיָהּ הַלְלוּ עַבְדֵי יהוה הַלְלוּ אֶת־שֵׁם יהוה.
יְהִי שֵׁם יהוה מְבֹרָךְ מֵעַתָּה וְעַד עוֹלָם.
מִמִּזְרַח־שֶׁמֶשׁ עַד מְבוֹאוֹ מְהֻלָּל שֵׁם יהוה.
רָם עַל כׇּל־גּוֹיִם יהוה עַל הַשָּׁמַיִם כְּבוֹדוֹ.
מִי כַּיהוה אֱלֹהֵינוּ הַמַּגְבִּיהִי לָשָׁבֶת.
הַמַּשְׁפִּילִי לִרְאוֹת בַּשָּׁמַיִם וּבָאָרֶץ.
מְקִימִי מֵעָפָר דָּל מֵאַשְׁפֹּת יָרִים אֶבְיוֹן.
לְהוֹשִׁיבִי עִם נְדִיבִים עִם נְדִיבֵי עַמּוֹ.
מוֹשִׁיבִי עֲקֶרֶת הַבַּיִת אֵם הַבָּנִים שְׂמֵחָה, הַלְלוּיָהּ.

Halleluyah! Cry praise, all you who serve the Eternal One,
praise the name of the Eternal One!

Let the name of the Eternal One be blessed,
henceforth and for eternity!

From east to west, sunrise to sunset,
hailed in every place: the name of God!

Raised up above all nations is the Eternal One,
Above even the heavens is God's glory!

Who is like the Eternal One our God?
Enthroned on high,

who gazes down on all,
in heaven and on earth,

who raises from the dust the poor,
from ash-heaps lifts aloft the needy,

placing them beside the privileged,
together with the privileged of the nation,

turning the childless household
into a home rejoicing in its children.
Halleluyah!

Psalm 113

Many verses of these psalms have been set to contemporary music because they were sung in the Temple at holy occasions. The experience of freedom at the seder is best appreciated through all our senses. The words of the psalms themselves remind us—"the mountains danced about like rams, the hills, like flocks of lambs." It is not enough to read the words; they are meant to be sung and danced. We rejoice with all of our faculties and our entire body. Like Miriam, we can lift our voices in song and our feet in dance at *Hallel*.
Barbara Penzner

בְּצֵאת יִשְׂרָאֵל מִמִּצְרָיִם בֵּית יַעֲקֹב מֵעַם לֹעֵז.
הָיְתָה יְהוּדָה לְקָדְשׁוֹ יִשְׂרָאֵל מַמְשְׁלוֹתָיו.
הַיָּם רָאָה וַיָּנֹס הַיַּרְדֵּן יִסֹּב לְאָחוֹר.
הֶהָרִים רָקְדוּ כְאֵילִים גְּבָעוֹת כִּבְנֵי צֹאן.
מַה לְּךָ הַיָּם כִּי תָנוּס הַיַּרְדֵּן תִּסֹּב לְאָחוֹר.
הֶהָרִים תִּרְקְדוּ כְאֵילִים גְּבָעוֹת כִּבְנֵי צֹאן.
מִלִּפְנֵי אָדוֹן חוּלִי אָרֶץ מִלִּפְנֵי אֱלוֹהַּ יַעֲקֹב.
הַהֹפְכִי הַצּוּר אֲגַם־מָיִם חַלָּמִישׁ לְמַעְיְנוֹ־מָיִם.

Betzeyt yisra'el mimitzrayim beyt ya'akov me'am lo'ez.
Hayetah yehudah lekodsho yisra'el mamshelotav.
Hayam ra'ah vayanos hayarden yisov le'aḥor.
Heharim rakedu ḥe'eylim geva'ot kivney tzon.
Ma leḥa hayam ki tanus hayarden tisov le'aḥor.
Heharim tirkedu ḥe'eylim geva'ot kivney tzon.
Milifney adon ḥuli aretz milifney eloha ya'akov.
Hahofḥi hatzur agam mayim ḥalamish lemayno mayim.

When Israel went forth out of Egypt,
House of Jacob from the people of a foreign tongue,

Judah became God's holy place,
Israel became God's seat of rule.

The sea beheld and fled,
the Jordan turned, reversed its flow.

The mountains danced about like rams,
the hills, like flocks of lambs.

What's wrong with you, O Sea, that you shall flee?
And you, O Jordan, that you turn around?

You mountains, why do you rejoice like rams,
you hills, like flocks of lambs?

Tremble, earth before the mighty one,
before the God of Jacob,

who turns the rock into a pool of water,
the flint into a bubbling fount!

Psalm 114

Gratitude is very important in the liberation process. Like acceptance, gratitude roots us in the present moment. It is a spiritual tool that frees us from the human tendency to suffer because of our unfulfilled desires and cravings. The bondage of dissatisfaction can be broken with praise and gratitude for what we have received. This unleashes energy, produces happiness, and leads to more gratitude.

Hallel is about praising God, not about self-satisfaction. The latter makes us complacent and lethargic, but the former can only expand our dedication to the principles that God's goodness represents in our lives. Our praise of God can motivate us to do God's work in the world—the work of liberation, love, and justice.
Sheila Peltz Weinberg

What is similar about mountains dancing like rams, the Jordan reversing its direction, and seas fleeing? How are these events like the parting of the sea?
Jeffrey Schrier

Lift the cup.

בָּרוּךְ אַתָּה יהוה אֱלֹהֵֽינוּ מֶֽלֶךְ הָעוֹלָם (נְבָרֵךְ אֶת רֽוּחַ
הָעוֹלָם) אֲשֶׁר גְּאָלָֽנוּ וְגָאַל אֶת־אֲבוֹתֵֽינוּ מִמִּצְרַֽיִם, וְהִגִּיעָֽנוּ
לַלַּֽיְלָה הַזֶּה לֶאֱכָל־בּוֹ מַצָּה וּמָרוֹר. כֵּן יהוה אֱלֹהֵֽינוּ
וֵאלֹהֵי אֲבוֹתֵֽינוּ, יַגִּיעֵֽנוּ לְמוֹעֲדִים וְלִרְגָלִים אֲחֵרִים הַבָּאִים
לִקְרָאתֵֽנוּ לְשָׁלוֹם, שְׂמֵחִים בְּבִנְיַן עִירֶֽךָ, וְשָׂשִׂים בַּעֲבוֹדָתֶֽךָ.
וְנוֹדֶה לְךָ שִׁיר חָדָשׁ עַל גְּאֻלָּתֵֽנוּ וְעַל פְּדוּת נַפְשֵֽׁנוּ. בָּרוּךְ
אַתָּה יהוה (נְבָרֵךְ אֶת רֽוּחַ הָעוֹלָם) גָּאַל יִשְׂרָאֵל.

Blessed are you, Eternal One our God, sovereign of all worlds
(**We bless the spirit of the world**), who has redeemed us and
our ancestors from Egypt, and has enabled us to reach this
night in order to eat matzah and *maror*. May you, Eternal One
our God and God of our ancestors, make it possible for us to
celebrate other holidays and festivals in peace, joyful in the re-
building of your city Jerusalem and happy in your service. We
will offer a new song of gratitude for our physical and spiritual liberation. Praised are you, Eternal One (**We bless the spirit
of the world**), redeemer of the people Israel.

We continue the process of liberation as we drink the second cup of wine. We have experienced the awareness of degradation that compelled the Israelites to resist enslavement. We drink this second cup in honor of redemption, even as we acknowledge the continuing struggle and the unknown road through the desert.

בָּרוּךְ אַתָּה יהוה אֱלֹהֵֽינוּ מֶֽלֶךְ הָעוֹלָם בּוֹרֵא פְּרִי הַגָּֽפֶן.

Baruḥ atah adonay eloheynu meleḥ ha'olam borey peri hagafen.

Blessed are you, Eternal One our God, sovereign of all worlds, who creates the fruit of the vine.

or

נְבָרֵךְ אֶת רֽוּחַ הָעוֹלָם בּוֹרֵאת פְּרִי הַגָּֽפֶן.

Nevareḥ et ruaḥ ha'olam boreyt peri hagafen.

We bless the spirit of the world, who creates the fruit of the vine.

Drink while reclining.

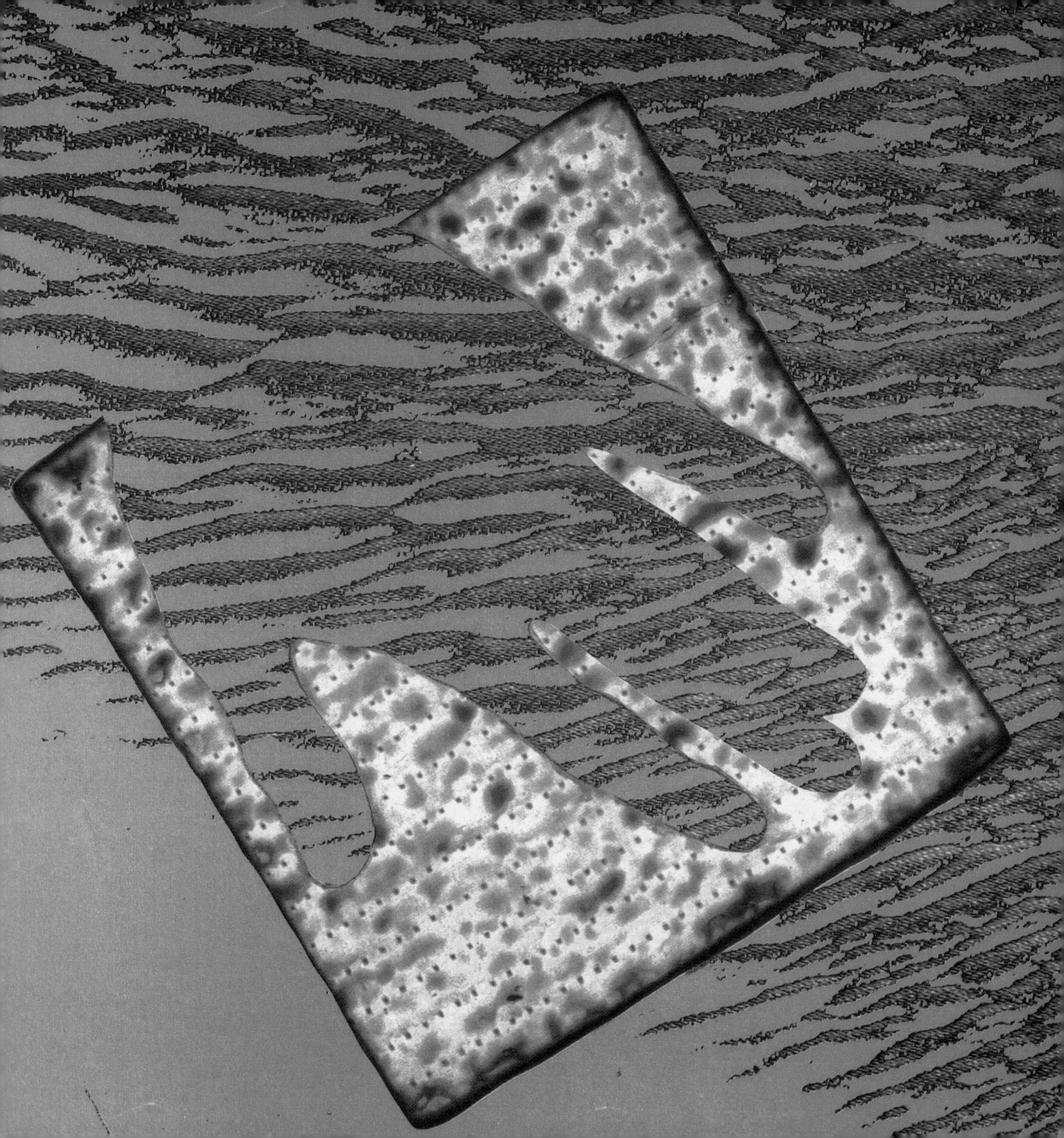

ROḤTZAH רחצה

HAND WASHING

It is customary to wash our hands before reciting *motzi*. This reflects an important early democratization within Judaism that occurred when the rabbis suggested that each home is a *mikdash me'at,* a small sanctuary. Just as the priests in the time of the Temple washed before making a meal offering on the altar, so do we wash before reciting *motzi* at our table. In taking on this priestly function in our own homes, we accept the challenge to create holiness in our homes just as it was up to the priests to guard the sanctity of the Temple.
David Teutsch

Once again we wash our hands, but much has changed since the seder began. We have passed through the long night of Egypt, and we stand on the far side of the Sea of Reeds. We now wash our hands to celebrate our crossing the sea, our rebirth as a free people. Now we recite a blessing, for our hands are free to perform acts of holiness, to eat matzah, the symbol of liberation.

In this moment of celebration, may this water, symbolically drawn from Miriam's well, cleanse us of all the wounds and pain of Egypt. For even as we remember the past, we are called to strive for a healing future.

Either have one person walk around the table with a pitcher of water and a basin or invite people to wash each other's hands.

בָּרוּךְ אַתָּה יהוה אֱלֹהֵינוּ מֶלֶךְ הָעוֹלָם אֲשֶׁר קִדְּשָׁנוּ
בְּמִצְוֹתָיו וְצִוָּנוּ עַל נְטִילַת יָדָיִם.

Baruḥ atah adonay eloheynu meleḥ ha'olam asher kideshanu bemitzvotav vetzivanu al netilat yadayim.

Blessed are you, Eternal One our God, sovereign of all worlds, who has made us holy with your *mitzvot* and commanded us to wash our hands.

or

נְבָרֵךְ אֶת רוּחַ הָעוֹלָם אֲשֶׁר קִדְּשַׁתְנוּ בְּמִצְוֹתֶיהָ וְצִוַּתְנוּ עַל
נְטִילַת יָדָיִם.

Nevareḥ et ruaḥ ha'olam asher kideshatnu bemitzvoteha vetzivatnu al netilat yadayim.

We bless the spirit of the world, who has made us holy with the *mitzvot* and commanded us to wash our hands.

In this illustration, the surrounding matzah creates the shape of a hand out of empty space. What deeds can fill the empty places in our world or in ourselves? How is tzedakah—the opportunity to perform acts of righteousness—like an outstretched hand? Jeffrey Schrier

מוֹצִיא מַצָּה

MOTZI MATZAH

BLESSING OVER MATZAH

רַבָּן גַּמְלִיאֵל הָיָה אוֹמֵר: כָּל שֶׁלֹּא אָמַר שְׁלֹשָׁה דְבָרִים
אֵלּוּ בַּפֶּסַח לֹא יָצָא יְדֵי חוֹבָתוֹ, וְאֵלּוּ הֵן:
מַצָּה, מָרוֹר וּפֶסַח.

Rabban Gamliel would say: "Those who have not explained three things during the seder have not fulfilled their obligation. These are matzah, *maror,* and the *pesaḥ* offering."

מַצָּה זוֹ, שֶׁאָנוּ אוֹכְלִים, עַל שׁוּם מָה? עַל שׁוּם שֶׁלֹּא
הִסְפִּיק בְּצֵקָם שֶׁל אֲבוֹתֵינוּ לְהַחֲמִיץ, עַד שֶׁנִּגְלָה עֲלֵיהֶם
מֶלֶךְ מַלְכֵי הַמְּלָכִים הַקָּדוֹשׁ בָּרוּךְ הוּא וּגְאָלָם, שֶׁנֶּאֱמַר:
וַיֹּאפוּ אֶת־הַבָּצֵק אֲשֶׁר הוֹצִיאוּ מִמִּצְרַיִם עֻגֹת מַצּוֹת, כִּי
לֹא חָמֵץ. כִּי גֹרְשׁוּ מִמִּצְרַיִם וְלֹא יָכְלוּ לְהִתְמַהְמֵהַּ, וְגַם
צֵדָה לֹא עָשׂוּ לָהֶם.

MATZAH: Why do we eat it? In order to remind ourselves that even before the dough of our ancestors could become leavened bread, the Holy One was revealed to the people and redeemed them, as it is written: "And they baked unleavened cakes of the dough that they had taken out of Egypt, for it was not leavened, since they had been driven out of Egypt and they could not delay; nor had they prepared any provisions for themselves." *Exodus 12:39*

Lift the three matzot *and say the following two blessings:*

בָּרוּךְ אַתָּה יהוה אֱלֹהֵֽינוּ מֶֽלֶךְ הָעוֹלָם הַמּוֹצִיא לֶֽחֶם מִן הָאָֽרֶץ.

Baruḥ atah adonay elo<u>hey</u>nu <u>me</u>leḥ ha'olam ha<u>mo</u>tzi <u>le</u>ḥem min ha'<u>a</u>retz.

Blessed are you, Eternal One our God, sovereign of all worlds, who brings forth bread from the earth.

The *motzi* blessing praises God for "bringing forth bread from the earth." But God only provides the raw materials: it is we who must plant, tend, harvest, and bake in order to create bread. Thus we learn that we are God's partners in the work of creation. *Richard Hirsh*

בָּרוּךְ אַתָּה יהוה אֱלֹהֵֽינוּ מֶֽלֶךְ הָעוֹלָם אֲשֶׁר קִדְּשָֽׁנוּ בְּמִצְוֹתָיו וְצִוָּֽנוּ עַל אֲכִילַת מַצָּה.

Baruḥ atah adonay elo<u>hey</u>nu <u>me</u>leḥ ha'olam asher kide<u>sha</u>nu bemitzvotav vetzi<u>va</u>nu al aḥilat matzah.

Blessed are you, Eternal One our God, sovereign of all worlds, who has made us holy with your *mitzvot* and commanded us to eat matzah.

Ordinarily we recite only one blessing over bread. Here there are two. The one said every day is in appreciation for the creation of the bread itself. The other is a recognition that at the seder we are required to eat matzah. Whereas all during the rest of Pesaḥ we can simply forego all leavened breads, we are required to eat matzah at the seder because it is a stand-in for the first Pesaḥ meal that signifies redemption. This shows itself in our tradition in many ways. Perhaps the most obvious is that the name for the blessing over bread is *motzi,* which is from the same root as *yitziah,* bringing forth or going forth. Bread is the symbol of the redemption embodied by food in our daily lives. Additionally, matzah symbolizes Pesaḥ redemption. *David Teutsch*

or

נְבָרֵךְ אֶת רֽוּחַ הָעוֹלָם הַמּוֹצִיאָה לֶֽחֶם מִן הָאָֽרֶץ.

Nevareḥ et <u>ru</u>aḥ ha'olam hamotziah <u>le</u>ḥem min ha'<u>a</u>retz.

We bless the spirit of the world, who brings forth bread from the earth.

Although we add a second blessing for matzah, the first blessing continues to speak of *<u>le</u>ḥem,* bread. Matzah isn't only a ritual food; it is also the "staff of life." *Robert Goldenberg*

נְבָרֵךְ אֶת רֽוּחַ הָעוֹלָם אֲשֶׁר קִדְּשַֽׁתְנוּ בְּמִצְוֹתֶֽיהָ וְצִוַּֽתְנוּ עַל אֲכִילַת מַצָּה.

Nevareḥ et <u>ru</u>aḥ ha'olam asher kide<u>shat</u>nu bemitzvo<u>te</u>ha vetzi<u>vat</u>nu al aḥilat matzah.

We bless the spirit of the world, who has made us holy with the *mitzvot* and commanded us to eat matzah.

Eat from the top and middle matzah while reclining.

We meet again after another year. You look much the same. With so many wrinkles on your face, you never seem to get any older. You never gain weight either, but then again, I couldn't imagine a fat matzah.

What is your secret? Why do we make a fuss about you? Unlike other *mitzvot,* it is not enough just to eat you; we must explain the whys and wherefores of matzah.

You seem so simple, plain, and flat. You would have been ignored by the palates of humanity except for your role in history. Your secret cannot be hidden inside of you, for there is no room, and with all those holes, everything is revealed. Your outsides and your insides are the same.

For a symbol of freedom, you are not very impressive. You do not sparkle like wine, you are not sweet like *ḥaroset,* or delicious and sumptuous like the festive meal. On this night of rejoicing, you are just your simple self. Shouldn't freedom have a more striking representative than you?

And even that symbolism is confusing. For you are not only the dough that our ancestors did not have time to let rise as they left Egypt. You are also the bread of affliction that our ancestors ate as slaves. You were the cheap but filling food given to satisfy the masses.

You were there from beginning to end. You who were the bread of slaves became the sustenance of a free people. From *leḥem oni* to *afikoman,* from slave past to messianic future. All the blows of the taskmasters can be seen on your pockmarked surface. Fragile as you are, you have survived unbroken. You remind us of our humble beginnings, and yet you show that the lowly can also become free. You are the symbol of the possibility of change for us all. You are the focal point of the Haggadah, for freedom is the dominion of the free—its gates are open to all. Yet free as you are, changed as you are, you are exactly the same as your slave self. For you watched yourself to prevent contamination with the yeast of pride, the lust for wealth, the thirst for praise. No leavening was allowed to puff you up artificially, to make you appear to be more than your natural self.

Simple, plain, and flat. Matzah, the eternal symbol of freedom, is the antithesis of fine food and wine, for freedom lies in the intoxication with the idea, not with the self.

Michael Strassfeld

MAROR מָרוֹר

BITTER HERBS

מָרוֹר זֶה שֶׁאָנוּ אוֹכְלִים עַל שׁוּם מָה? עַל שׁוּם שֶׁמֵּרְרוּ
הַמִּצְרִים אֶת־חַיֵּי אֲבוֹתֵינוּ בְּמִצְרַיִם, שֶׁנֶּאֱמַר: וַיְמָרְרוּ
אֶת־חַיֵּיהֶם בַּעֲבֹדָה קָשָׁה, בְּחֹמֶר וּבִלְבֵנִים וּבְכָל עֲבֹדָה
בַּשָּׂדֶה, אֵת כָּל־עֲבֹדָתָם אֲשֶׁר עָבְדוּ בָהֶם בְּפָרֶךְ.

MAROR: Why do we eat it? To remind ourselves that the Egyptians made life bitter for our ancestors in Egypt, as it is written, "Ruthlessly, they made life bitter for them with harsh labor at mortar and bricks, and with all sorts of tasks in the field." *Exodus 1:14*

Take maror, *dip it in* ḥaroset *and recite:*

בָּרוּךְ אַתָּה יהוה אֱלֹהֵינוּ מֶלֶךְ הָעוֹלָם אֲשֶׁר קִדְּשָׁנוּ
בְּמִצְוֹתָיו וְצִוָּנוּ עַל אֲכִילַת מָרוֹר.

Baruḥ atah adonay eloheynu meleḥ ha'olam asher kideshanu bemitzvotav vetzivanu al aḥilat maror.

Blessed are you, Eternal One our God, sovereign of all worlds, who has made us holy with *mitzvot* and commanded us to eat *maror.*

or

נְבָרֵךְ אֶת רוּחַ הָעוֹלָם אֲשֶׁר קִדְּשַׁתְנוּ בְּמִצְוֹתֶיהָ וְצִוַּתְנוּ עַל
אֲכִילַת מָרוֹר.

Nevareḥ et ruaḥ ha'olam asher kideshatnu bemitzvoteha vetzivatnu al aḥilat maror.

We bless the spirit of the world, who has made us holy with *mitzvot* and commanded us to eat *maror.*

Eat the maror *with the* ḥaroset.

Rabbi Bunam said: "We eat the seder meal in the following order: the matzah first, and the bitter herbs next, though it would seem the reverse order is proper, since we first suffered and later were freed. The reason for this, however, is that as long as there was no prospect of being redeemed, the Israelites did not feel keenly the bitterness of their lot. But as soon as Moses spoke to them of freedom, they awoke to the bitterness of their slavery." *Michael Strassfeld*

Ḥaroset, because of its color and texture, is usually explained as symbolic of the mortar we were forced to make as slaves. On the other hand, its sweetness is meant to offset the bitterness of the *maror.* It is also suggested that the apples in the *ḥaroset* are to remind us of the apple trees in the fields under which the Hebrew women in Egypt gave birth. According to a *midrash,* the women would give birth in the fields and leave the children there so that the Egyptians would not find them and drown them in the river. *Michael Strassfeld*

There are many customary recipes for *ḥaroset* that reflect the many lands in which Jews have lived. Some Jews use figs and dates. A few even include a piece of earth to remind us of the mortar in a direct way. *David Teutsch*

From darkness to light, from slavery to freedom, from winter to spring, and now from bitterness to sweetness. But with the light, there is still darkness in the world. With our freedom, there are still those who are enslaved. It is still winter for some, and life remains bitter for many throughout our world.

Even in our own lives, we live within the tapestry of these contradictions. It is dark, and it is light; we are trapped, and we are liberated; we are cold, and we are warm; we experience pain and joy, just as we have eaten the *maror* with the *ḥaroset,* taking the bitter with the sweet.

Through this act, we acknowledge the fullness of life, shaded by the gradations of experience; never black and white but a reflection of the full range of possibilities.

Joy Levitt

KOREḤ כורך

EATING MATZAH AND BITTER HERBS TOGETHER

The original *koreḥ* combined the three basic symbols of Pesaḥ into one sandwich. When the Temple was destroyed and the pascal lamb was no longer available, another piece of matzah was substituted. When we recognize that the pascal lamb and the matzah are both redemption symbols, it is easy to understand the substitution. *David Teutsch*

Can we outdo Hillel? What other foods and symbols would we put between the *matzot* to create the most comprehensive story-of-slavery sandwich one could imagine? *Jeffrey Schein*

The pascal sacrifice seems far away from us today. But try to imagine that this represented the annual gathering of Jews who were celebrating religious independence and hoping for national liberation. Hundreds of thousands of Jews would come to Jerusalem to proclaim the hope for redemption. This was our ancient "Independence Day." *Naamah Kelman*

Take pieces of the bottom matzah and make a sandwich with maror *in the middle and say:*

זֵכֶר לְמִקְדָּשׁ כְּהִלֵּל: כֵּן עָשָׂה הִלֵּל בִּזְמַן שֶׁבֵּית הַמִּקְדָּשׁ
הָיָה קַיָּם. הָיָה כּוֹרֵךְ מַצָּה וּמָרוֹר וְאוֹכֵל בְּיַחַד, לְקַיֵּם מַה
שֶּׁנֶּאֱמַר: עַל מַצּוֹת וּמְרֹרִים יֹאכְלֻהוּ.

As a reminder of the sacrificial system in the Temple in Jerusalem, we observe the practice of Hillel. In the days when the Temple was still standing, Hillel would make a sandwich with matzah and *maror* and eat it, in order to fulfill the verse, "They shall eat it with *matzot* and *maror.*" *Numbers 9:11*

פֶּסַח שֶׁהָיוּ אֲבוֹתֵינוּ אוֹכְלִים בִּזְמַן שֶׁבֵּית הַמִּקְדָּשׁ הָיָה
קַיָּם, עַל שׁוּם מָה? עַל שׁוּם שֶׁפָּסַח הַקָּדוֹשׁ בָּרוּךְ הוּא עַל
בָּתֵּי אֲבוֹתֵינוּ בְּמִצְרַיִם, שֶׁנֶּאֱמַר: וַאֲמַרְתֶּם זֶבַח פֶּסַח הוּא
לַיהוה, אֲשֶׁר פָּסַח עַל בָּתֵּי בְנֵי יִשְׂרָאֵל בְּמִצְרַיִם, בְּנָגְפּוֹ
אֶת־מִצְרַיִם, וְאֶת־בָּתֵּינוּ הִצִּיל.

PESAḤ: Why did our ancestors eat the *pesaḥ* offering during the time of the Temple? As a reminder that the Holy One protected the houses of our ancestors in Egypt, as it is written: "You shall say, 'It is the *pesaḥ* sacrifice to the Eternal One, because God passed over the houses of the Israelites in Egypt when God smote the Egyptians, but saved our houses.'" *Exodus 12:27*

Eat the maror *sandwich while reclining, as we remember the* pesaḥ *offering in ancient times.*

What is the significance of the *pesaḥ*, the pascal lamb? On the night before they were to leave Egypt, the Israelites were told to slaughter a lamb and paint their doorposts with its blood, a sign to the destroying angel not to take the first born in those homes. Today we no longer sacrifice an animal, but we do remember that night of terror and hope, a prelude to redemption. That night, as people huddled in their homes awaiting the morning, perhaps they thought: "Will the promise to punish the slave masters be fulfilled, or will morning come and leave us exposed, having marked ourselves as rebellious slaves?" The *pesaḥ* is a reminder that freedom begins when we mark our doors, when we take the risk of speaking up and standing out. Saying no to oppression, being open and proud of our Judaism, allowing ourselves to be fully who we are, daring to believe that things will be different—this is how we mark ourselves as a people on the road to liberation. *Toba Spitzer*

שלחן עורך

SHULḤAN OREḤ

THE MEAL IS SERVED

Below are several readings on the theme of freedom that you may wish to discuss during the meal. The seder continues on page 89.

Freedom is not merely a matter of choice, of personal whim. Freedom is not an artifact, an expedient for more efficient social management. Freedom is at the core of life, at the heart of the human personality.

Ira Eisenstein

Liberation is costly. Even after the Lord had delivered the Israelites from Egypt, they had to travel through the desert. They had to bear the responsibilities and difficulties of freedom. There was starvation and thirst and they kept complaining. They complained that their diet was monotonous. Many of them preferred the days of bondage and the fleshpots of Egypt.

We must remember that liberation is costly. It needs unity. We must hold hands and refuse to be divided. We must be ready. Some of us will not see the day of our liberation physically. But those people will have contributed to the struggle. Let us be united, let us be filled with hope. Let us be those who respect one another.

Desmond Tutu

The freedom of this meal at which all are equally free is expressed in a number of rites which "distinguish this night from all nights." . . . This particular freedom expresses itself in the fact that the youngest child is the one to speak, and that what the father says at the table is adapted to this child's personality and degree of maturity. In contrast to all instruction, which is necessarily autocratic and never on the basis of equality, the sign of a true and free social intercourse is this, that the one who stands—relatively speaking—nearest the periphery of the circle gives the cue for the level on which the conversation is to be conducted. For this conversation must include everyone. . . . The freedom of a society is always the freedom of everyone who belongs to it.

Franz Rosenzweig

So pharaonic oppression, deliverance, Sinai, and Canaan are still with us, powerful memories shaping our perceptions of the political world. The "door of hope" is still open; things are not what they might be—even when what they might be isn't totally different from what they are. . . . We still believe, or many of us do, what the Exodus first taught, or what it has commonly been taken to teach, about the meaning and possibility of politics and about its proper form:

—first, that wherever you live, it is probably Egypt;

—second, that there is a better place, a world more attractive, a promised land;

—and third, that "the way to the land is through the wilderness." There is no way to get from here to there except by joining together and marching.

Michael Walzer

We are the magicians
it is more than staff into snake we seek.

We dream a sentence into life

We must.

We are skilled in the kitchen
of language and longing
baking leftover letters
into nourishment
for our hungry.

Miriam you are our finest

patchwork kittel
dusty scraps from history's cutting floor
silk like grandmother's lips
and new truths ablaze
with laughing
and the murmur of girls
studying Talmud and dance

Miriam we kiss your fringes
gulp down the water
we bless with your name

Miriam, on this night we are free
Five thousand years of desert
and now everywhere wells.

Tamara Cohen

TZAFUN צפון

EATING THE AFIKOMAN

After the meal, eat the afikoman *while reclining.*

???

One of the most unusual aspects of the seder is that it can't continue until the children find the *afikoman*. This means that the kids have a lot of power. Can you think of other times when children have that much power? Why did the people who made up the seder want to make children so important in it?
Sheila Peltz Weinberg

When some of us were children, this moment was the high point of the seder. This was the time we would search for (and always find) the *afikoman,* a portion of the middle matzah that had been hidden at the beginning of the seder. We knew that the seder could not be completed until the *afikoman* had been found and redeemed with gifts so that everyone could be given a piece to nibble for dessert.

Even as children, we knew that it wasn't possible to find everything that was missing in life. As much as we prized the gift we received for our bargaining, it was the hunt that we really loved, running through the rooms and turning everything upside down.

The older we get, the harder the search becomes. We aren't always sure now what we are seeking, what the *afikoman* means to us, which dessert will bring us a sense of completion and satisfaction. Unlike during our childhood search, there are now fewer loving and reliable coaches in the next room giving us clues. There are no guarantees that we will find what we are looking for. But this we know: it is still the search that is important—the looking, the running, and the turning everything upside down.

Joy Levitt

The *pesaḥ* offering was eaten at the end of the meal when people were almost satiated. In remembrance of this, we eat the *afikoman* at the end of the meal. Derived from a Greek word of uncertain meaning, *afikoman* probably means either dessert after the meal or the practice of going reveling from house to house after the meal. The rabbis forbade this ancient equivalent of party-hopping because it was not in keeping with the sacredness of the seder. They also wanted the taste of the *pesaḥ* offering to linger in the mouth, so nothing was eaten during the seder after the *afikoman*.
Michael Strassfeld

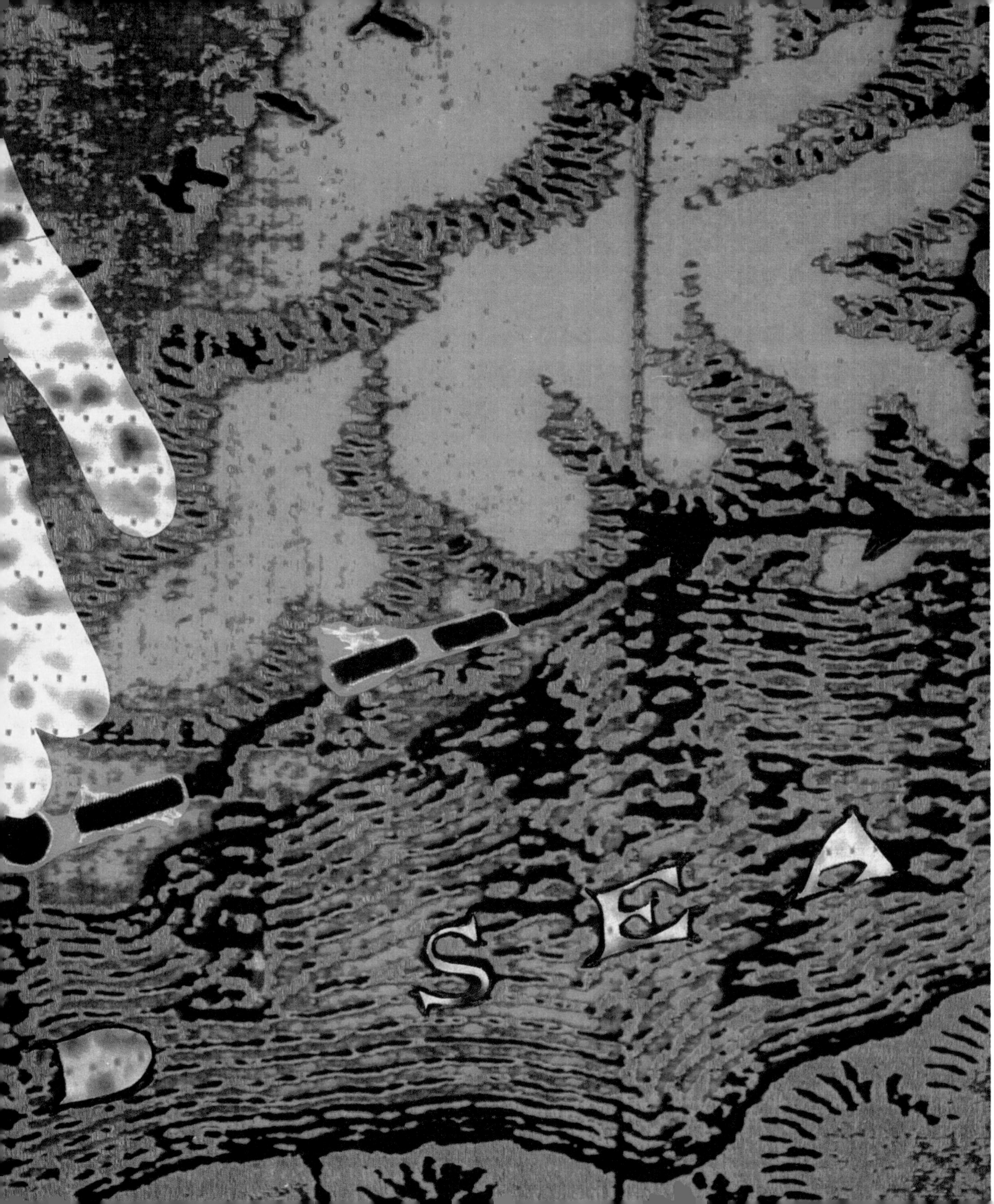
SEA

SEA OF
REEDS

BAREḤ ברך

GRACE AFTER MEALS

Recite either the traditional version of Grace after Meals below or an alternative on page 98.

שִׁיר הַמַּעֲלוֹת בְּשׁוּב יהוה אֶת־שִׁיבַת צִיּוֹן הָיִינוּ
כְּחֹלְמִים. אָז יִמָּלֵא שְׂחוֹק פִּינוּ וּלְשׁוֹנֵנוּ רִנָּה. אָז יֹאמְרוּ
בַגּוֹיִם הִגְדִּיל יהוה לַעֲשׂוֹת עִם־אֵלֶּה. הִגְדִּיל יהוה
לַעֲשׂוֹת עִמָּנוּ הָיִינוּ שְׂמֵחִים. שׁוּבָה יהוה אֶת־שְׁבִיתֵנוּ
כַּאֲפִיקִים בַּנֶּגֶב. הַזֹּרְעִים בְּדִמְעָה בְּרִנָּה יִקְצֹרוּ. הָלוֹךְ יֵלֵךְ
וּבָכֹה נֹשֵׂא מֶשֶׁךְ־הַזָּרַע בֹּא־יָבֹא בְרִנָּה נֹשֵׂא אֲלֻמֹּתָיו.

Shir hama'alot beshuv adonay et shivat tziyon hayinu keḥolmim. Az yimaley seḥok pinu ulshonenu rinah. Az yomeru vagoyim higdil adonay la'asot im eleh. Higdil adonay la'asot imanu hayinu semeḥim. Shuvah adonay et shevitenu ka'afikim banegev. Hazorim bedimah berinah yiktzoru. Haloḥ yeleḥ uvaḥoh nosey mesheḥ hazara bo yavo verinah nosey alumotav.

A reaching up song.
We will be like dreamers
When the Eternal One brings us back to Zion.
Then we will laugh again. Then we will sing again.
Then will it be said abroad: "Great is what the Eternal One did for them!"
The Eternal One will do great things for us, and we shall rejoice.
Eternal One, bring us back! As you bring back water to dried-up Negev streams.
We who sowed with tears will reap with song.
When the sowers cast their seeds they feel like weeping.
Yet they go on trusting that they will come back.
They will surely come back singing when they bring in the harvests' sheaves.

When ten or more adults are present, include the word (eloheynu).

Leader: חֲבֵרַי נְבָרֵךְ.

All: יְהִי שֵׁם יהוה מְבֹרָךְ מֵעַתָּה וְעַד עוֹלָם.

Leader: יְהִי שֵׁם יהוה מְבֹרָךְ מֵעַתָּה וְעַד עוֹלָם.
בִּרְשׁוּת חֲבֵרַי נְבָרֵךְ (אֱלֹהֵינוּ) שֶׁאָכַלְנוּ מִשֶּׁלוֹ.

All: בָּרוּךְ (אֱלֹהֵינוּ) שֶׁאָכַלְנוּ מִשֶּׁלוֹ וּבְטוּבוֹ חָיִינוּ.

Leader: בָּרוּךְ (אֱלֹהֵינוּ) שֶׁאָכַלְנוּ מִשֶּׁלוֹ וּבְטוּבוֹ חָיִינוּ.

All: בָּרוּךְ הוּא וּבָרוּךְ שְׁמוֹ.

Leader: *Ḥaveray nevareḥ.*
All: *Yehi shem adonay mevoraḥ me'atah ve'ad olam.*
Leader: *Yehi shem adonay mevoraḥ me'atah ve'ad olam. Birshut ḥaveray nevareḥ (eloheynu) she'aḥalnu mishelo.*
All: *Baruḥ (eloheynu) she'aḥalnu mishelo uvtuvo ḥayinu.*
Leader: *Baruḥ (eloheynu) she'aḥalnu mishelo uvtuvo ḥayinu.*
All: *Baruḥ hu uvaruḥ shemo.*

Leader: Friends, let us give thanks!
All: May the name of the Eternal One be praised now and always.
Leader: May the name of the Eternal One be praised now and always. With your consent: We praise (our God) the one whose food we have eaten.
All: Praised is (our God) the one whose food we have eaten and by whose goodness we live.
Leader: Praised is (our God) the one whose food we have eaten and by whose goodness we live.
All: Praised be God and praised be God's name.

Praise is yours, Eternal One our God, ruler of all, who every day invites the world to a feast of goodness, compassion, and love. You feed us, you sustain us. You overwhelm us with your goodness. You provide for all. You love endlessly. Because you are so good to us, we never lacked sustenance in the past. And we hope that we will never lack food in the future. This you do for your own renown, that we may know you as the one who sustains and supports all and prepares the food each creature needs. Blessed are you, Eternal One, who sustains all.

So we thank you, Eternal One our God, because you granted our ancestors a land desirable, good and wide. And you extricated us, Eternal One our God, from the straits of Egypt. You freed us from being at home in servitude. And for the promise you sealed within our flesh. And for the Torah—teaching that you impart to us. And for the limits of conduct that you made us know. And for life, for beauty, for love, with which you are so generous. And for the joy of eating that you allow us, all the while nourishing us every day, every moment.

For all this, Eternal One our God, we thankfully confess and worship you, whose name is praised by ever new expressions of life. We do this as Torah states: "Eat your fill praising the Eternal One your God for the earthly goodness that God freely gave you." Therefore we say: "Blessed are you, Eternal One, for the land and for the food."

Be loving, Eternal One our God, to Israel your folk, Jerusalem your city, and Zion your glory's shrine. Remember David's throne and the holy house, the Temple of grandeur where it was so easy to call on you.

God, parent, provider, sustainer, you nourish and support us and keep us independent. Eternal One our God, keep us free from needs that enslave us. Permit us not to depend on human handouts or loans. But may we depend on your full, yet broadly open holy hand. Always spare us shame and disgrace.

בָּרוּךְ אַתָּה יהוה אֱלֹהֵינוּ מֶלֶךְ הָעוֹלָם הַזָּן אֶת הָעוֹלָם כֻּלּוֹ בְּטוּבוֹ בְּחֵן בְּחֶסֶד וּבְרַחֲמִים. הוּא נוֹתֵן לֶחֶם לְכָל-בָּשָׂר כִּי לְעוֹלָם חַסְדּוֹ. וּבְטוּבוֹ הַגָּדוֹל תָּמִיד לֹא חָסַר לָנוּ וְאַל יֶחְסַר-לָנוּ מָזוֹן לְעוֹלָם וָעֶד בַּעֲבוּר שְׁמוֹ הַגָּדוֹל. כִּי הוּא אֵל זָן וּמְפַרְנֵס לַכֹּל וּמֵטִיב לַכֹּל וּמֵכִין מָזוֹן לְכָל-בְּרִיּוֹתָיו אֲשֶׁר בָּרָא. בָּרוּךְ אַתָּה יהוה הַזָּן אֶת הַכֹּל.

נוֹדֶה לְךָ יהוה אֱלֹהֵינוּ עַל-שֶׁהִנְחַלְתָּ לַאֲבוֹתֵינוּ אֶרֶץ חֶמְדָּה טוֹבָה וּרְחָבָה וְעַל-שֶׁהוֹצֵאתָנוּ יהוה אֱלֹהֵינוּ מֵאֶרֶץ מִצְרַיִם וּפְדִיתָנוּ מִבֵּית עֲבָדִים. וְעַל-בְּרִיתְךָ שֶׁחָתַמְתָּ בִּלְבֵנוּ וְעַל-תּוֹרָתְךָ שֶׁלִּמַּדְתָּנוּ וְעַל-חֻקֶּיךָ שֶׁהוֹדַעְתָּנוּ וְעַל-חַיִּים חֵן וָחֶסֶד שֶׁחוֹנַנְתָּנוּ. וְעַל-אֲכִילַת מָזוֹן שָׁאַתָּה זָן וּמְפַרְנֵס אוֹתָנוּ תָּמִיד בְּכָל-יוֹם וּבְכָל-עֵת וּבְכָל-שָׁעָה.

וְעַל-הַכֹּל יהוה אֱלֹהֵינוּ אֲנַחְנוּ מוֹדִים לָךְ וּמְבָרְכִים אוֹתָךְ יִתְבָּרַךְ שִׁמְךָ בְּפִי כָל-חַי תָּמִיד לְעוֹלָם וָעֶד. כַּכָּתוּב וְאָכַלְתָּ וְשָׂבָעְתָּ וּבֵרַכְתָּ אֶת-יהוה אֱלֹהֶיךָ עַל-הָאָרֶץ הַטּוֹבָה אֲשֶׁר נָתַן-לָךְ. בָּרוּךְ אַתָּה יהוה עַל-הָאָרֶץ וְעַל-הַמָּזוֹן.

רַחֵם יהוה אֱלֹהֵינוּ עַל-יִשְׂרָאֵל עַמֶּךָ וְעַל-יְרוּשָׁלַיִם עִירֶךָ וְעַל-צִיּוֹן מִשְׁכַּן כְּבוֹדֶךָ וְעַל-מַלְכוּת בֵּית דָּוִד מְשִׁיחֶךָ וְעַל-הַבַּיִת הַגָּדוֹל וְהַקָּדוֹשׁ שֶׁנִּקְרָא שִׁמְךָ עָלָיו.

אֱלֹהֵינוּ אָבִינוּ רְעֵנוּ זוּנֵנוּ פַּרְנְסֵנוּ וְכַלְכְּלֵנוּ וְהַרְוִיחֵנוּ וְהַרְוַח-לָנוּ יהוה אֱלֹהֵינוּ, מְהֵרָה מִכָּל-צָרוֹתֵינוּ; וְנָא אַל-תַּצְרִיכֵנוּ יהוה אֱלֹהֵינוּ לֹא לִידֵי מַתְּנַת בָּשָׂר וָדָם וְלֹא לִידֵי הַלְוָאָתָם כִּי-אִם לְיָדְךָ הַמְּלֵאָה הַפְּתוּחָה הַקְּדוֹשָׁה וְהָרְחָבָה שֶׁלֹּא נֵבוֹשׁ וְלֹא נִכָּלֵם לְעוֹלָם וָעֶד.

On Shabbat

[In commanding us, Eternal One our God, you impart to us the strength to fulfill the mitzvah. We thank you for the mitzvah of the seventh day, the great Shabbat, the Holy Shabbat, this Shabbat. A great and holy day it is. It is a day in which we live your presence. We rest in it, we relax in it, loving you all the more for the limits you have set on our actions by your will. On this day of rest, Eternal One our God, may there be no pain, no worry, no oppression, no anxiety and no sighing. On this Shabbat day, Eternal One our God, open our eyes to the vision of the consolation of Zion and the upbuilding of Jerusalem. For you are at liberty to freely give salvation and consolation.]

Our God, our ancients' God, may our prayer rise and come to you, and be beheld, and be acceptable. Let it be heard, acted upon, remembered—the memory of us and all our needs, the memory of our ancestors, the memory of messianic hopes, the memory of Jerusalem your holy city, and the memory of all your kin, the house of Israel, all surviving in your presence. Act for goodness and grace, for love and care, for life, well-being, and peace, on this day of the festival of *matzot*. Remember us this day, Eternal One our God, for goodness. Favor us this day with blessing. Preserve us this day for life. With your redeeming, nurturing word, be kind and generous. Act tenderly on our behalf, and grant us victory over all our trials. Truly, our eyes are turned toward you, for you are a providing God; gracious and merciful are you.

Make this world a place of holiness, now in our lifetime as you rebuild Jerusalem. Blessed are you, Eternal One, who in building up mercy builds Jerusalem. Amen!

On Shabbat

[רְצֵה וְהַחֲלִיצֵנוּ יהוה אֱלֹהֵינוּ בְּמִצְוֹתֶיךָ וּבְמִצְוַת יוֹם הַשְּׁבִיעִי הַשַּׁבָּת הַגָּדוֹל וְהַקָּדוֹשׁ הַזֶּה. כִּי יוֹם זֶה גָּדוֹל וְקָדוֹשׁ הוּא לְפָנֶיךָ לִשְׁבָּת בּוֹ וְלָנוּחַ בּוֹ בְּאַהֲבָה כְּמִצְוַת רְצוֹנֶךָ. וּבִרְצוֹנְךָ הָנִיחַ לָנוּ יהוה אֱלֹהֵינוּ שֶׁלֹּא תְהִי צָרָה וְיָגוֹן וַאֲנָחָה בְּיוֹם מְנוּחָתֵנוּ. וְהַרְאֵנוּ יהוה אֱלֹהֵינוּ בְּנֶחָמַת צִיּוֹן עִירֶךָ וּבְבִנְיַן יְרוּשָׁלַיִם עִיר קָדְשֶׁךָ. כִּי אַתָּה הוּא בַּעַל הַיְשׁוּעוֹת וּבַעַל הַנֶּחָמוֹת.]

אֱלֹהֵינוּ וֵאלֹהֵי אֲבוֹתֵינוּ וְאִמּוֹתֵינוּ יַעֲלֶה וְיָבֹא וְיַגִּיעַ וְיֵרָאֶה וְיֵרָצֶה וְיִשָּׁמַע וְיִפָּקֵד וְיִזָּכֵר זִכְרוֹנֵנוּ וּפִקְדוֹנֵנוּ וְזִכְרוֹן אֲבוֹתֵינוּ וְאִמּוֹתֵינוּ וְזִכְרוֹן יְמוֹת מָשִׁיחַ צִדְקֶךָ וְזִכְרוֹן יְרוּשָׁלַיִם עִיר קָדְשֶׁךָ וְזִכְרוֹן כָּל עַמְּךָ בֵּית יִשְׂרָאֵל לְפָנֶיךָ לִפְלֵיטָה וּלְטוֹבָה לְחֵן וּלְחֶסֶד וּלְרַחֲמִים לְחַיִּים וּלְשָׁלוֹם בְּיוֹם חַג הַמַּצּוֹת הַזֶּה. זָכְרֵנוּ יהוה אֱלֹהֵינוּ בּוֹ לְטוֹבָה וּפָקְדֵנוּ בוֹ לִבְרָכָה וְהוֹשִׁיעֵנוּ בוֹ לְחַיִּים. וּבִדְבַר יְשׁוּעָה וְרַחֲמִים חוּס וְחָנֵּנוּ וְרַחֵם עָלֵינוּ וְהוֹשִׁיעֵנוּ כִּי אֵלֶיךָ עֵינֵינוּ כִּי אֵל מֶלֶךְ חַנּוּן וְרַחוּם אָתָּה.

וּבְנֵה יְרוּשָׁלַיִם עִיר הַקֹּדֶשׁ בִּמְהֵרָה בְיָמֵינוּ. בָּרוּךְ אַתָּה יהוה בֹּנֵה בְרַחֲמָיו יְרוּשָׁלָיִם אָמֵן.

Blessed are you, Eternal One our God, sovereign though hidden. Day by day you do good according to that day's needs. So you did act out of your goodness and so you will deal well with us in the future. You give of yourself, you gave of yourself, you will give of yourself, freely to us, completely, and kindly, mercifully and abundantly, to save us, to prosper us, to bless us, to redeem us, to console us, to sustain and support us, in mercy, life, and goodness, while not diminishing the good you hold in store for us for eternity.

Kind One, rule us always.
Caring One, be involved in our heaven and in our earth.
Loving One, praised by each generation to the next, take pride in us always. May our lives honor you in this world and in the next.
Merciful One, let us earn in an honorable way.
Liberating One, break the restraints that make us strangers. Lead us home with dignity.
Generous One, send abundant blessedness to this home and to this table.
Compassionate One! Bless the State of Israel with Jerusalem its holy city. Bring full redemption to them both.
Compassionate One! Create a caring bond between the children of Sarah and the children of Hagar.
Compassionate One! Send redemption to all Jews who suffer privation or captivity.
God of pleasant surprises, how blessed it is to remember Elijah the prophet. Send to us soon the good news of redemption and consolation.

May the all-merciful bless me, (my wife, my husband, my children, my father, my mother, my beloved, my hosts) all who are gathered here and all we have.

All of us be blessed like Abraham, blessed in everything; like Isaac, blessed by everyone; like Jacob, blessed in every way with the blessing of completeness. And like Sarah,

בָּרוּךְ אַתָּה יהוה אֱלֹהֵינוּ מֶלֶךְ הָעוֹלָם הָאֵל אָבִינוּ מַלְכֵּנוּ אַדִּירֵנוּ בּוֹרְאֵנוּ גֹּאֲלֵנוּ יוֹצְרֵנוּ קְדוֹשֵׁנוּ קְדוֹשׁ יַעֲקֹב רוֹעֵנוּ רוֹעֵה יִשְׂרָאֵל. הַמֶּלֶךְ הַטּוֹב וְהַמֵּטִיב לַכֹּל שֶׁבְּכָל־יוֹם וָיוֹם הוּא הֵטִיב הוּא מֵטִיב הוּא יֵטִיב לָנוּ. הוּא גְמָלָנוּ הוּא גוֹמְלֵנוּ הוּא יִגְמְלֵנוּ לָעַד לְחֵן לְחֶסֶד וּלְרַחֲמִים וּלְרֶוַח הַצָּלָה וְהַצְלָחָה בְּרָכָה וִישׁוּעָה נֶחָמָה פַּרְנָסָה וְכַלְכָּלָה וְרַחֲמִים וְחַיִּים וְשָׁלוֹם וְכָל־טוֹב וּמִכָּל־טוּב לְעוֹלָם אַל־יְחַסְּרֵנוּ.

הָרַחֲמָן הוּא יִמְלֹךְ עָלֵינוּ לְעוֹלָם וָעֶד. הָרַחֲמָן הוּא יִתְבָּרַךְ בַּשָּׁמַיִם וּבָאָרֶץ. הָרַחֲמָן הוּא יִשְׁתַּבַּח לְדוֹר דּוֹרִים וְיִתְפָּאַר בָּנוּ לָנֶצַח נְצָחִים וְיִתְהַדַּר בָּנוּ לָעַד וּלְעוֹלְמֵי עוֹלָמִים. הָרַחֲמָן הוּא יְפַרְנְסֵנוּ בְּכָבוֹד. הָרַחֲמָן הוּא יִשְׁבֹּר עֻלֵּנוּ מֵעַל־צַוָּארֵנוּ וְהוּא יוֹלִיכֵנוּ קוֹמְמִיּוּת לְאַרְצֵנוּ. הָרַחֲמָן הוּא יִשְׁלַח בְּרָכָה מְרֻבָּה בַּבַּיִת הַזֶּה וְעַל־שֻׁלְחָן זֶה שֶׁאָכַלְנוּ עָלָיו. הָרַחֲמָן הוּא יְבָרֵךְ אֶת מְדִינַת יִשְׂרָאֵל עִם יְרוּשָׁלַיִם עִיר הַקֹּדֶשׁ וִיבִיאֵן לִגְאֻלָּה שְׁלֵמָה. הָרַחֲמָן הוּא יִתֵּן אַחֲוָה בֵּין בְּנֵי שָׂרָה וּבֵין בְּנֵי הָגָר. הָרַחֲמָן הוּא יִשְׁלַח גְּאֻלָּה לְכָל יִשְׂרָאֵל הַנְּתוּנִים בְּצָרָה וּבְשִׁבְיָה. הָרַחֲמָן הוּא יִשְׁלַח לָנוּ אֶת־אֵלִיָּהוּ הַנָּבִיא זָכוּר לַטּוֹב וִיבַשֶּׂר־לָנוּ בְּשׂוֹרוֹת טוֹבוֹת יְשׁוּעוֹת וְנֶחָמוֹת.
הָרַחֲמָן הוּא יְבָרֵךְ אוֹתִי
(וְאֶת־אִשְׁתִּי
וְאֶת־אִישִׁי
וְאֶת־זַרְעִי
וְאֶת־אָבִי מוֹרִי
וְאֶת־אִמִּי מוֹרָתִי
וְאֶת־רֵעִי/רַעְיָתִי
וְאֶת־בַּעַל/בַּעֲלַת/בַּעֲלֵי הַבַּיִת הַזֶּה)
וְאֶת־כָּל־הַמְסוּבִּין כָּאן
וְאֶת־כָּל־אֲשֶׁר לָנוּ.
כְּמוֹ שֶׁנִּתְבָּרְכוּ אֲבוֹתֵינוּ אַבְרָהָם יִצְחָק וְיַעֲקֹב בַּכֹּל מִכֹּל כֹּל וְאִמּוֹתֵינוּ שָׂרָה רִבְקָה רָחֵל וְלֵאָה כֵּן יְבָרֵךְ אוֹתָנוּ כֻּלָּנוּ יַחַד בִּבְרָכָה שְׁלֵמָה וְנֹאמַר אָמֵן.

blessed with fruit in her old age; like Rebekah, blessed by her courage and conviction; like Rachel, blessed in love and wisdom; like Leah, blessed by inner sight. To this we say Amen.

Eternal One, interpret our deeds as flowing from good intentions, worthy of blessing from you. Helping God, accept our act of thanksgiving as a favor on your part. May we be found pleasant and wise by you and by our comrades.

On Shabbat

[Compassionate One! Anchor us and settle us, so that our true home be established in time that is altogether Shabbat, in space that is altogether tranquil, and in life that is altogether alive.]

Compassionate One! Make this day altogether good!

Compassionate One! Enable us to move toward messianic days, toward a perfected world. May your sovereignty shine in the world. Help us live so that we be worthy of the messianic days and the coming world. God! We know that you make peace on high. Grant peace to us and to all Israel. Jews live in many lands, among many nations who also need peace. Grant us peace.

Revere the Eternal One, you who make God holy! Revering only God, what will you lack?

Those who are self-sufficient like young lions may starve in relying on their own strength. But those who seek only the Eternal One—they will not miss all that is good. Thank the Eternal One, who is so good, whose kindness is ever in the world, whose will it is for hands to open and satisfy all who live. Blessed are they who trust in the Eternal One, who will be their trust. May what we ate be a source of satisfaction, what we drank a source of health, what we left a source of blessing. According to Torah, "Food was set before them, they ate, and some was left, as the Eternal One had spoken." The Eternal One will surely give strength to this folk. The Eternal One will bless this folk with shalom.

בַּמָּרוֹם יְלַמְּדוּ עֲלֵיהֶם וְעָלֵינוּ זְכוּת שֶׁתְּהִי לְמִשְׁמֶרֶת שָׁלוֹם וְנִשָּׂא בְרָכָה מֵאֵת יהוה וּצְדָקָה מֵאֱלֹהֵי יִשְׁעֵנוּ. וְנִמְצָא־חֵן וְשֵׂכֶל טוֹב בְּעֵינֵי אֱלֹהִים וְאָדָם.

On Shabbat

[הָרַחֲמָן הוּא יַנְחִילֵנוּ יוֹם שֶׁכֻּלּוֹ שַׁבָּת וּמְנוּחָה לְחַיֵּי הָעוֹלָמִים.] הָרַחֲמָן הוּא יַנְחִילֵנוּ יוֹם שֶׁכֻּלּוֹ טוֹב. הָרַחֲמָן הוּא יְזַכֵּנוּ לִימוֹת הַמָּשִׁיחַ וּלְחַיֵּי הָעוֹלָם הַבָּא.

מִגְדּוֹל יְשׁוּעוֹת מַלְכּוֹ וְעֹשֶׂה־חֶסֶד לִמְשִׁיחוֹ לְדָוִד וּלְזַרְעוֹ עַד־עוֹלָם. עוֹשֶׂה שָׁלוֹם בִּמְרוֹמָיו הוּא יַעֲשֶׂה שָׁלוֹם עָלֵינוּ וְעַל־כָּל־יִשְׂרָאֵל וְעַל כָּל־יוֹשְׁבֵי תֵבֵל וְאִמְרוּ אָמֵן.

יְראוּ אֶת־יהוה קְדֹשָׁיו כִּי אֵין מַחְסוֹר לִירֵאָיו. כְּפִירִים רָשׁוּ וְרָעֵבוּ וְדֹרְשֵׁי יהוה לֹא־יַחְסְרוּ כָל־טוֹב. הוֹדוּ לַיהוה כִּי־טוֹב כִּי לְעוֹלָם חַסְדּוֹ. פּוֹתֵחַ אֶת־יָדֶךָ וּמַשְׂבִּיעַ לְכָל־חַי רָצוֹן. בָּרוּךְ הַגֶּבֶר אֲשֶׁר יִבְטַח בַּיהוה וְהָיָה יהוה מִבְטַחוֹ.

מַה־שֶּׁאָכַלְנוּ יִהְיֶה לְשָׂבְעָה וּמַה־שֶּׁשָּׁתִינוּ יִהְיֶה לִרְפוּאָה וּמַה־שֶּׁהוֹתַרְנוּ יִהְיֶה לִבְרָכָה כְּדִכְתִיב וַיִּתֵּן לִפְנֵיהֶם וַיֹּאכְלוּ וַיּוֹתִירוּ כִּדְבַר יהוה.

יהוה עֹז לְעַמּוֹ יִתֵּן יהוה יְבָרֵךְ אֶת־עַמּוֹ בַשָּׁלוֹם.

AN ALTERNATIVE BLESSING AFTER THE MEAL

בְּרִיךְ רַחֲמָנָא מַלְכָּא דִי עָלְמָא מָרֵיהּ דְהַאי פִּיתָּא.

Beriḥ raḥamana malka de'alma marey dehay pita.

You are the source of life for all that is and your blessing flows through me.

Interpretative blessing after meals by Shefa Gold, based on Beraḥot 40b.

THE THIRD CUP

We dedicated the first cup of wine to awareness—the first step taken in the journey toward liberation. We drank the second cup in celebration of the redemption from Egypt. We now drink this third cup in gratitude for all the gifts we have been given. The seder reminds us of the gifts of relationships—of friends and family; and of our material possessions—good food and drink. Yet most of all we offer thanks for the greatest gift—the ability to challenge, to question, to choose, and therefore to strive for freedom.

Lift the cup and recite:

בָּרוּךְ אַתָּה יהוה אֱלֹהֵינוּ מֶלֶךְ הָעוֹלָם בּוֹרֵא פְּרִי הַגָּפֶן.

Baruḥ atah adonay eloheynu meleḥ ha'olam borey peri hagafen.

Blessed are you, Eternal One our God, sovereign of all worlds, who creates the fruit of the vine.

or

נְבָרֵךְ אֶת רוּחַ הָעוֹלָם בּוֹרֵאת פְּרִי הַגָּפֶן.

Nevareḥ et ruaḥ ha'olam boreyt peri hagafen.

We bless the spirit of the world, who creates the fruit of the vine.

Drink while reclining.

SEFIRAT HA'OMER ספירת העומר
COUNTING THE OMER

Only recited on the second night.

On the second day of Pesaḥ in ancient times, our ancestors brought the first sheaf of barley reaped that season as an offering to God. From that day, they began counting the days and weeks to Shavuot, when they would celebrate the beginning of the wheat harvest by offering loaves made of the first wheat. Even after the Temple was destroyed and offerings were no longer brought, Jews have continued to count the days from Pesaḥ to Shavuot in accordance with the biblical injunction.

Thus our ancestors linked Pesaḥ and Shavuot as occasions for thanking God for the fruits of the field. So do we thank God for the renewal of life that all nature proclaims at this season.

בָּרוּךְ אַתָּה יהוה אֱלֹהֵינוּ מֶלֶךְ הָעוֹלָם (נְבָרֵךְ אֶת רוּחַ הָעוֹלָם) אֲשֶׁר קִדְּשָׁנוּ בְּמִצְוֹתָיו וְצִוָּנוּ עַל סְפִירַת הָעֹמֶר.

Baruḥ atah adonay eloheynu meleḥ ha'olam (***Nevareḥ et ruaḥ ha'olam***) *asher kideshanu bemitzvotav vetzivanu al sefirat ha'omer.*

Blessed are You, Eternal One our God, sovereign of all worlds (**We bless the spirit of the world**) who has made us holy with your *mitzvot,* and commanded us concerning the counting of the Omer.

הַיּוֹם יוֹם אֶחָד לָעֹמֶר.

Hayom yom eḥad la'omer

Today is the first day of the Omer.

After the Temple was destroyed, Shavuot became the annual celebration of the giving (that is, the acceptance) of the Torah, and the counting of the Omer became a vigil. Mere release from slavery felt incomplete. If life has no transcendent value, "freedom" by itself has no meaning. *Robert Goldenberg*

Freedom in Jewish tradition is always yoked to responsibility. Freedom is not some abstract concept—it contains specific obligations, spelled out in detail in the stories, texts, and traditions of our people. Beginning with the second night of Pesaḥ, we mark the period of seven weeks that link Pesaḥ to Shavuot through the counting of the Omer.

Shavuot, celebrating the receiving of the Torah at Mount Sinai, is the necessary complement to Pesaḥ, for it alerts us to what may be the essential paradox of the Haggadah: that our ancestors, in escaping slavery in Egypt, willingly accepted the servitude of Sinai. Our ancestors used their newfound freedom to choose whom they would serve, how they would serve, and the means by which they would serve. *Richard Hirsh*

This section offers seder participants an opportunity to expand on the story of the Exodus by exploring more contemporary experiences of slavery and liberation. *For a shorter seder, turn to page 118 for the Cups of Miriam and Elijah.*

בכל־דור ודור

BEḤOL DOR VADOR
IN EVERY GENERATION

In every generation, each individual should feel personally redeemed from Egypt. Whoever expands upon the story of the ongoing Exodus is worthy of praise.

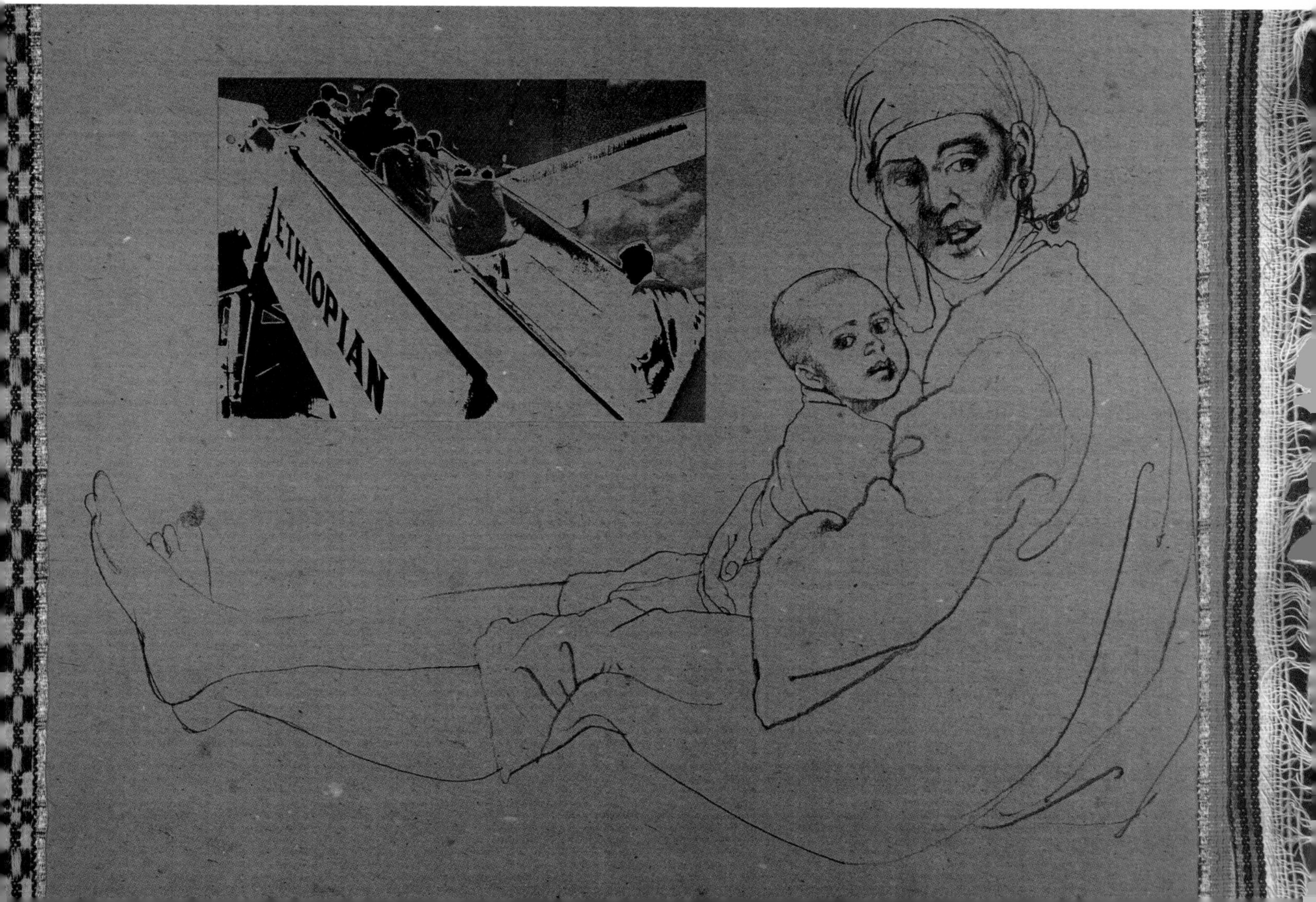

Another explanation of this story has come to light in the recent archeological excavation of the underground caves where Rabbi Akiva and his followers hid. They literally could not see the light of day, so students were sent out to look for the sunlight and announce the time for reciting the *Shema*.
Naamah Kelman

מַעֲשֶׂה בְּרַבִּי אֱלִיעֶזֶר וְרַבִּי יְהוֹשֻׁעַ וְרַבִּי אֶלְעָזָר בֶּן־עֲזַרְיָה וְרַבִּי עֲקִיבָא וְרַבִּי טַרְפוֹן, שֶׁהָיוּ מְסֻבִּין בִּבְנֵי בְרַק, וְהָיוּ מְסַפְּרִים בִּיצִיאַת מִצְרַיִם כָּל־אוֹתוֹ הַלַּיְלָה, עַד שֶׁבָּאוּ תַלְמִידֵיהֶם וְאָמְרוּ לָהֶם: רַבּוֹתֵינוּ, הִגִּיעַ זְמַן קְרִיאַת שְׁמַע שֶׁל שַׁחֲרִית.

A story is told about Rabbi Eliezer, Rabbi Joshua, Rabbi Elazar ben Azariah, Rabbi Akiva, and Rabbi Tarfon. They were at a seder in Benei Brak, and they were relating the story of the Exodus from Egypt throughout the night. Their students finally interrupted them, saying, "Our teachers, the time has come to recite the morning *Shema*."

The story continues—it repeats itself again and again. After the Exodus and Sinai, we wander in the desert on our way to the promised land. Tonight we visit some of those places on the continuing journey from Exodus to liberation.

אֵלֶּה מַסְעֵי בְנֵי יִשְׂרָאֵל אֲשֶׁר יָצְאוּ מֵאֶרֶץ מִצְרָיִם.
וַיִּסְעוּ בְנֵי יִשְׂרָאֵל מֵרַעְמְסֵס וַיַּחֲנוּ בְּסֻכֹּת.
וַיִּסְעוּ מִסֻּכֹּת וַיַּחֲנוּ בְאֵתָם.
וַיִּסְעוּ מֵאֵתָם וַיַּחֲנוּ בְּבָבֶל.
וַיִּסְעוּ מִבָּבֶל וַיַּחֲנוּ בִּסְפָרַד.
וַיִּסְעוּ... וַיַּחֲנוּ... בְּצָרְפַת...
בִּצְפוֹן אַפְרִיקָה... בְּאַשְׁכְּנַז...
בְּפוֹלִין... בְּרוּסְיָה... בְּאַמֵרִיקָה...
אֵלֶּה מַסְעֵי בְנֵי יִשְׂרָאֵל.

These are the wanderings of the people Israel after they went out of Egypt.
And Israel traveled from Ramses and camped in Sukkot.
They traveled from Sukkot and camped in Eitam.
They traveled from Eitam and camped in Babylon.
They traveled from Babylon and camped in Spain.
They traveled . . . they camped . . . in France,
in North Africa, in Germany, in Poland, in Russia,
in the Americas. . . .
These are the wanderings of the people Israel.

וְכָל־הַמַּרְבֶּה לְסַפֵּר בִּיצִיאַת מִצְרַיִם, הֲרֵי זֶה מְשֻׁבָּח.

Whoever expands upon the story of the Exodus is worthy of praise.

One way to understand this little story (especially its place after the injunction to expand on the story of the Exodus), is that it underscores the importance of the mitzvah to tell the story as thoroughly as possible. Even the sages, who presumably knew the story, were obliged to retell it during the seder. In fact, they spent so much time discussing it that they were unaware that morning had arrived. Another explanation suggests that this group of rabbis, which included Rabbi Akiva, was plotting the revolt of Bar Koḥba against the Romans in the year 132 C.E. Perhaps the students' statement was actually a warning that the Romans were arriving.
Michael Strassfeld

Can you describe how Ethiopian Jews may have felt as they turned from the land of their birth to board planes for Israel? What do you know of their new lives? Is freedom always experienced as a blessing?
Jeffrey Schrier

MAGGID

The courage to let go of the door, the handle.
The courage to shed the familiar walls whose very
stains and leaks are comfortable as the little moles
of the upper arm, stains that recall a feast,
a child's naughtiness, a loud blattering storm
that slapped the roof hard, pouring through.

The courage to abandon the graves dug into the hill,
the small bones of children and the brittle bones
of the old whose marrow hunger had stolen;
the courage to desert the tree planted and only begun
 to bear,
the riverside where promises were shaped;
the street where their empty pots were broken.

The courage to leave the place whose language you
 learned
as early as your own, whose customs however dangerous
or demeaning, bind you like a halter
you have learned to pull inside, to move your load;
the land fertile with the blood spilled on it;
the roads mapped and annotated for survival.

The courage to walk out of the pain that is known
into the pain that cannot be imagined,
mapless, walking into the wilderness, going
barefoot with a canteen into the desert;
stuffed in the stinking hold of a rotting ship
sailing off the map into dragon's mouths,

Cathay, India, Siberia, *goldeneh medina,*
leaving bodies by the way like abandoned treasure.
So they walked out of Egypt. So they bribed their way
out of Russia under loads of straw, so they steamed
out of the bloody smoking charnel house of Europe
on overloaded freighters forbidden all ports.

Out of pain into death or freedom or a different
painful dignity, into squalor and politics.
We Jews are all born of wanderers, with shoes
under our pillows and a memory of blood that is ours
raining down. We honor only those Jews who changed
  tonight
those who chose the desert over bondage,

who walked into the strange and became strangers
and gave birth to children who could look down
on them standing on their shoulders for having
been slaves. We honor those who let go of everything but
freedom, who ran, who revolted, who fought,
who became other by saving themselves.

Marge Piercy

Overleaf:
This illustration is a reinterpretation of a painting from a third-century synagogue in Syria known as the Dura Europus. In this form, the illustration depicts the infant Moses being taken from the bulrushes merged with a picture of a child being taken captive by Nazi soldiers. Why do you think this image is entitled Children of the Bulrushes?
Jeffrey Schrier

וְהִיא שֶׁעָמְדָה לַאֲבוֹתֵֽינוּ וְלָֽנוּ. שֶׁלֹּא אֶחָד בִּלְבָד עָמַד עָלֵֽינוּ לְכַלּוֹתֵֽנוּ. אֶלָּא שֶׁבְּכָל־דּוֹר וָדוֹר עוֹמְדִים עָלֵֽינוּ לְכַלּוֹתֵֽנוּ. וְהַקָּדוֹשׁ בָּרוּךְ הוּא מַצִּילֵֽנוּ מִיָּדָם.

Vehi she'amdah vehi she'amdah la'avoteynu velanu (2)
shelo eḥad bilvad amad aleynu leḥaloteynu (2)
ela shebeḥol dor vador omdim aleynu leḥaloteynu (2)
Vehakadosh baruḥ hu matzileynu miyadam. (2)

This promise has been reliable for our ancestors and ourselves, for not only was there once an enemy that tried to destroy us. In every generation there have been those who wished to destroy us, but the Holy One rescues us from their hands.

The text of the Haggadah asserts that God has always saved us from our enemies; the following reading is a response to that notion.

We recited the customary blessings, the Psalms, and to finish we sang *Ḥad Gadya,* that terrifying song in which, in the name of justice, evil catches evil, death calls death, until the angel of destruction, in his turn, has his throat cut by the Eternal. I loved this naive little song in which everything seemed so simple, so primitive: the cat and the dog, the water and the fire, executioners and victims turn and turn about, all undergoing the same punishment inside the same scheme. But that evening the song upset me. I rebelled against the resignation it implied. Why does God always act too late? Why didn't God get rid of the Angel of Death before he even committed his first murder?

Elie Wiesel

Elie Wiesel's narrative about Ḥad Gadya is portrayed here by the atom bomb, goose-stepping soldiers, and the Nazi stamp mark that includes a winged swastika. Why were smeared doorposts contrasted with clock parts? What might these symbols mean in relation to the passage of time and instances of prejudice?
Jeffrey Schrier

Our ability to live in freedom is due to those who came before us, who dared to dream of a better, freer place and journeyed across the ocean to countries that promised safety and liberation for all peoples. Choose one of the readings below, or tell your own stories.

As labor is the common burden of our race, so the effort of some to shift their share of the burden onto the shoulders of others is the great, durable, curse of the race. As I would not be a slave, so I would not be a master. This expresses my idea of democracy. Whatever differs from this, to the extent of the difference, is no democracy. Our reliance is in our love for liberty; our defense is in the spirit which prizes liberty as the heritage of all people in all lands everywhere. Destroy this spirit, and we have planted the seeds of despotism at our own doors.

Those who deny freedom to others deserve it not for themselves, and cannot long retain it. Why should there not be a patient confidence in the ultimate justice of the people? Is there any better or equal hope in the world?

Let us have faith that right makes might, and in that faith, let us, to the end, dare to do our duty as we understand it.

Abraham Lincoln

THE NEW COLOSSUS

Not like the brazen giant of Greek fame,
With conquering limbs astride from land to land;
Here at our sea-washed, sunset gates shall stand
A mighty woman with a torch, whose flame
Is the imprisoned lightning, and her name
Mother of Exiles. From her beacon-hand
Glows world-wide welcome; her mild eyes command
The air-bridged harbor that twin cities frame.
"Keep, ancient lands, your storied pomp!" cries she
With silent lips. "Give me your tired, your poor,
Your huddled masses yearning to breathe free,
The wretched refuse of your teeming shore.
Send these, the homeless, tempest-tossed to me,
I lift my lamp beside the golden door!"

Emma Lazarus

What do the Statue of Liberty and a Menorah have in common? Jeffrey Schrier

O FREEDOM

O Freedom, O freedom, O freedom over me
And before I'd be a slave
I'll be buried in my grave
And go home to my Lord and be free.

No more moaning, no more moaning, no more moaning
  over me
And before I'd be a slave
I'll be buried in my grave
And go home to my Lord and be free.

There'll be singing . . .
There'll be peace . . .

וְכָל־הַמַּרְבֶּה לְסַפֵּר בִּיצִיאַת מִצְרַיִם, הֲרֵי זֶה מְשֻׁבָּח.

Whoever expands upon the story of the Exodus is worthy of praise.

The inquisitive child asks, "How has the experience of living in North America been liberating for the Jewish people?"

The challenging child asks, "How has the experience of living in North America been bad for the Jewish people?"

The simple child asks, "Is our country still welcoming new immigrants from troubled lands?"

The confused child looks around at the homeless man lying in the street, the undocumented refugee living in fear of deportation, the hunger and poverty, and worries about the limits of democracy and the price of freedom.

The next selections include Jewish responses to the Holocaust. Choose one of the following three readings.

Pesaḥ is over. There were seders in the kosher kitchen. . . . At the second seder, I spoke briefly: To be a Jew means in every instance to be on a high plane. The temporary suffering and blows that descend upon the Jew have a meaning, are not merely oppressions, and do not degrade the Jew. For a Jew is part of a sacred triad: Israel, the Torah, and the Holy One. That means the Jewish people, the moral law, and the Creator of the universe. This sacred triad courses through history. It is a reality that has been tested countless times. Our grandfathers clung to the triad, lived by its strength.

To be sure, history rages now, a war is waged against the Jews, but the war is not only against one member of the triad but against the entire one: against the Torah and God, against the moral law and the Creator. Can anyone still doubt which side is stronger? In a war it happens that one regiment is defeated, taken into captivity. Let the ghetto Jews consider themselves as such prisoners of war. But let them also remember that the army as a whole is not defeated and cannot be defeated. The Pesaḥ of Egypt is a symbol of ancient victory of the sacred triad. My wish is that together we shall live to see the Pesaḥ of the future.

Zelig Kalmanovitsh, leader of the Vilna Ghetto

The Jews of Bergen-Belsen had no *matzot* for Pesaḥ in 1944. It was decided that the eating of leaven was permissible and that the following *kavanah* should be recited before meals:

"Our Father in Heaven, behold it is evident and known to you that it is our desire to do your will and to celebrate the Festival of Pesaḥ by eating matzah and by observing the prohibition of *ḥametz*. But our hearts are pained that the enslavement prevents us from eating matzah, and we are in danger of our lives. Behold we are ready to fulfill your commandment: 'And you shall live by them and not die by them.' Therefore, our prayer to you is that you may keep us alive and save us and rescue us speedily so that we may observe your commandments and do your will and serve you with a perfect heart. Amen."

On the eve of Pesaḥ 1943, the Jews of the Warsaw ghetto staged a revolt against the Nazis that lasted for forty-two days. Below is an account from the diary of the Commander of the Jewish Fighting Organization.

It is now clear to me that what took place exceeded all expectations. Our opposition to the Germans was greater than our strength allowed—but now our forces are waning. We are on the brink of extinction. We forced the Germans to retreat twice—but they returned stronger than before. . . . I feel that great things are happening and that this action which we have dared to take is of enormous value. I cannot describe the conditions in which the Jews of the ghetto are now "living." Only a few exceptional individuals will be able to survive such suffering. The others will sooner or later die. Their fate is certain, even though thousands are trying to hide in cracks and rat holes. It is impossible to light a candle, for lack of air. Greetings to you who are outside. Perhaps a miracle will occur and we shall see each other again one of these days. It is extremely doubtful.

The last wish of my life has been fulfilled. Jewish self-defense has become a fact. Jewish resistance and revenge have become actualities. I am happy to have been one of the first Jewish fighters in the ghetto.

From where will rescue come?

Mordechai Anielevitch

The following song was sung by many Jews during the Holocaust.

אֲנִי מַאֲמִין בֶּאֱמוּנָה שְׁלֵמָה בְּבִיאַת הַמָּשִׁיחַ. וְאַף עַל פִּי שֶׁיִּתְמַהְמֵהַּ, עִם כָּל־זֶה אֲחַכֶּה לוֹ בְּכָל־יוֹם שֶׁיָּבֹא.

Ani ma'amin (3) be'emunah sheleymah
bevi'at hamashiaḥ (2) ani ma'amin
Ve'af 'al pi sheyitmameyah
Im kol zeh ani ma'amin.

I believe with complete faith in the coming of the Messiah, and even though the Messiah may tarry, I still wait every day for the Messiah to come.

וְכָל־הַמַּרְבֶּה לְסַפֵּר בִּיצִיאַת מִצְרַיִם, הֲרֵי זֶה מְשֻׁבָּח.

Whoever expands upon the story of the Exodus is worthy of praise.

The silent child, in the face of all that has occurred, remains silent. There aren't even words locked up inside the silent one. The other children, by their silence, concur.

The founding of the State of Israel is the fulfillment of a dream that is thousands of years old. The following selections express both the hopes for and the challenges inherent in its creation. Choose one reading.

We hereby proclaim the establishment of the Jewish State in Palestine, to be called Israel. . . .

The State of Israel will promote the development of the country for the benefit of all its inhabitants; will be based on precepts of liberty, justice and peace taught by the Hebrew prophets; will uphold the full social and political equality of all its citizens without distinction of race, creed or sex; will guarantee full freedom of conscience, worship, education and culture.

Israeli Declaration of Independence, 1948

We tend to forget those days before the Six-Day War, and perhaps rightly so—yet those were the days in which we came closest to that Jewish fate from which we have run like haunted beings all these years. Suddenly, everyone was talking about Munich, about the Holocaust, about the Jewish people being left to its fate. A new holocaust did not seem as real a possibility to us as it did to the people of Europe; for us it was a concrete picture of an enemy victory, and we had decided that, come what might, we would prevent it. We know the meaning of genocide, both those of us who saw the Holocaust and those who were born later. Perhaps this is why the world will never understand our courage or comprehend the doubts and the qualms of conscience we knew during and after the war. Those who survived the Holocaust know that no other people carries with it such haunting visions. And it is these visions that compel us to fight and yet make us ashamed of our fighting. The saying, "Pardon us for winning" is no irony—it is the truth. Of course, one may say that our doubts are only hypocrisy and nothing more; that we deck ourselves out in morality, perhaps even that our behavior is contradictory. But who says that war can be anything but contradictory?

Our feelings are mixed. We carry in our hearts an oath that binds us never to return to the Europe of the Holocaust; but at the same time we do not wish to lose that Jewish identity with the victims.

Muki Tzur

Attending school in Haifa, I would have longed to visit my aunt's home, but she had fled to Lebanon during the fighting; she thought she was going for no more than a few weeks, but when the war ended, she was not allowed back.

One of my school friends was a Jewish girl named Devora. One day, she invited me home. When we neared her house, I suddenly realized where she was taking me: her family now occupied my aunt's house! My shock was redoubled when I went inside and found my aunt's pictures still hanging on the walls; it was on my aunt's piano that Devora practiced. I even found a doll I used to play with.

When I told Devora, she was as shocked as I. "Take your doll!" she exclaimed. "Let's be friends!" She explained that her family had received this house from the government on arriving in Israel. "We came from Poland; we were also refugees. We lost everything. All our relations died in the concentration camps." Later, she showed me the Auschwitz number tattooed on her mother's arm. "I'm very sorry we took over your aunt's home," she said, "But try to understand—if we hadn't come here, we would have all ended up in the gas ovens."

I bore no resentment against Devora or her parents. I sensed that they, too, felt the injustice of occupying someone else's home. "Soon the Arab refugees will be allowed to return to their homes," they reassured me, "and our government will build new houses for us . . . and then Jews and Arabs will live together in peace."

They were as naive as I: neither they nor I knew the true intentions of their government. My aunt was never permitted to return, and Devora's family remained in that house for twenty-five years.

Raymonda Tawil

HATIKVAH

כָּל עוֹד בַּלֵּבָב פְּנִימָה
נֶפֶשׁ יְהוּדִי הוֹמִיָּה
וּלְפַאֲתֵי מִזְרָח קָדִימָה
עַיִן לְצִיּוֹן צוֹפִיָּה
עוֹד לֹא אָבְדָה תִּקְוָתֵנוּ
הַתִּקְוָה מִשְּׁנוֹת אַלְפַּיִם
לִהְיוֹת עַם חָפְשִׁי בְּאַרְצֵנוּ
בְּאֶרֶץ צִיּוֹן וִירוּשָׁלַיִם.

Kol od balevav penimah
Nefesh yehudi homiyah
Ulefa'atey mizraḥ kadimah
Ayin letziyon tzofiyah
Od lo avedah tikvatenu
Hatikvah mishenot alpayim
Lihyot am ḥofshi be'artzenu
Be'eretz tziyon
virushalayim.

So long as a Jewish soul still lives within a heart,
And so long as an eye gazes longingly to Zion in the far reaches of the East,
Then the hope is not lost,
The hope of two thousand years,
That we may be a free people in our land,
Land of Zion and Jerusalem.

Naftali Hertz Imber,
translated by Judith Kaplan Eisenstein

וְכָל־הַמַּרְבֶּה לְסַפֵּר בִּיצִיאַת מִצְרַיִם, הֲרֵי זֶה מְשֻׁבָּח.

Whoever expands upon the story of the Exodus is worthy of praise.

The wise child asks, "Is the State of Israel finally our last redemption?"

The wicked child asks, "Have the oppressed become the oppressors?"

The simple child asks, "Is liberation always so costly?"

The silent child hears the voices of the refugees who have found a new home and so becomes hopeful for those who are not yet at home.

This section concludes with the echo of the rabbis of Beney Brak, where the section began.

The voices echoed all through the long night, until Elijah, the eternal student of humanity, entered and said, "Dawn is finally breaking, a new day is at hand, at last God's unity is complete. Therefore we should all recite the *Shema.*"

Rabbi Elazar ben Azariah said, "Behold I am nearly seventy years old, and I never understood why it was a mitzvah to remember the Exodus *at night.* After all, the verse says: 'In order that you may remember the *day* of your going out of Egypt all the *days* of your life'" *(Deuteronomy 16:3).*

Then Ben Zoma explained it to me: "'The *days* of your life' refers to the good times in the daylight—for then it is easy to remember. But when we sit in the darkness of fear so heavy that none can move, when we lose our firstborn, or when we know of others under the chain of oppression, how then can we talk of freedom? Because the verse reads '*all* the days of your life,' thereby teaching that both in darkness and in light, we remember Egypt. We remember freedom *and* slavery for the two are always mixed together."

The sages added: "'The days of your life' means in this world, but '*all* the days of your life' means to help bring about the messianic days." To remember is not enough; rather, one should work to help bring about a time when all are free.

Michael Strassfeld

כוס מרים   כוס אליהו

THE CUPS OF MIRIAM AND ELIJAH
DRAWING FROM THE PRESENT / WAITING FOR THE FUTURE

Lift Miriam's Cup and recite:

In the years of wandering in the desert, Miriam's well accompanied the Israelites. According to tradition, Miriam's well is still with us. Every Saturday night, at the end of Shabbat, its waters flow out into wells everywhere in the world.

While the return of Elijah is left to the future and all its potential, Miriam is present with us always. She is here to provide healing, inspiration, and wisdom. She and her waters sustain us as we await Elijah.

There is still a long journey to freedom, a long while before Elijah can herald the messianic age. Miriam the prophet calls us to work for—not wait for—that day.

She sustains us with the most basic substance on earth—water that cleanses and heals. She lifts our hearts as she leads us once again in song and dance.

Elijah's cup remains untouched by us. But we now drink from Miriam's cup, the nurturing waters of Miriam's well.

בָּרוּךְ אַתָּה יהוה אֱלֹהֵינוּ מֶלֶךְ הָעוֹלָם שֶׁהַכֹּל נִהְיֶה בִּדְבָרוֹ.

Baruḥ atah adonay eloheynu meleḥ ha'olam shehakol nihyeh bidvaro.

Praised are you, Eternal One our God, sovereign of all worlds, who creates all things.

or

נְבָרֵךְ אֶת רוּחַ הָעוֹלָם שֶׁהַכֹּל נִהְיֶה בִּדְבָרֶהָ.

Nevareḥ et ruaḥ ha'olam shehakol nihyeh bidvareha.

We bless the spirit of the world, who creates all things.

Everyone sips from Miriam's Cup as it is passed around the table.

Sing either Miriam Hanevi'ah *or* Ushavtem Mayim

מִרְיָם הַנְּבִיאָה עֹז וְזִמְרָה בְּיָדָהּ
מִרְיָם תִּרְקוֹד אִתָּנוּ לְהַגְדִּיל זִמְרַת עוֹלָם
מִרְיָם תִּרְקוֹד אִתָּנוּ לְתַקֵּן אֶת־הָעוֹלָם.
בִּמְהֵרָה בְיָמֵינוּ הִיא תְּבִיאֵנוּ
אֶל מֵי הַיְשׁוּעָה.

Leila Gal Berner

Miriam hanevi'ah oz vezimrah beyadah.
Miriam tirkod itanu lehagdil zimrat olam
Miriam tirkod itanu letaken et ha'olam.
Bimherah veyameynu hi tevi'enu
el mey hayeshu'ah. (2)

Miriam, so brave and strong
Prophetess of light and song
Miriam, come dance among us
To heal the world and right its wrongs.
Translation by Margot Stein

וּשְׁאַבְתֶּם מַּיִם בְּשָׂשׂוֹן
מִמַּעַיְנֵי הַיְשׁוּעָה.

Ushavtem mayim besason mima'ayney hayeshu'ah (2)
Mayim (4) hey mayim besason
Mayim (4) hey mayim besason
Hey (4) mayim (6) besason
Mayim (6) besason

Joyfully shall you pour water from the springs of righteous victory.

THE CUP OF ELIJAH כוס אליהו

The first Pesaḥ was observed while our ancestors were still slaves. It was enacted on the night of the tenth plague, when the firstborn of the Egyptians were killed. Both the locus and the focus of that first Pesaḥ is the doorway, the boundary that separates the circle of protection inside the Israelite dwellings from the destroying force that is ravaging Egypt.

But unlike the night of the first Pesaḥ, when to open the door was to invite disaster, we now confidently and deliberately throw open the door. In fact, as if to emphasize the distance we have traveled from Egypt, we send those who, on that first Pesaḥ night, would have been most vulnerable—our children—to the spot where they would have been most exposed, namely, the doorway.
Richard Hirsh

Fill the fourth cup. Everyone pours a little from their cups into Elijah's Cup. It will require all our efforts to bring about redemption. We stand as the door is opened for Elijah.

We open our doors and our hearts to welcome Elijah to our homes. Elijah, the eternal wanderer, is given a momentary respite and a drink from his cup before continuing his endless quest for the end of days. Elijah, the eternal companion of the Jewish people, will herald the messianic age. In the meantime, he reminds us of the hope he carries. He reappears at moments when that hope is tangible—at the seder and at the birth of children.

There are two visions described by the prophets Jeremiah and Malaḥi—one national and one personal:

לָכֵן הִנֵּה־יָמִים בָּאִים נְאֻם־יהוה וְלֹא יֵאָמֵר עוֹד־חַי יהוה
אֲשֶׁר הֶעֱלָה אֶת־בְּנֵי יִשְׂרָאֵל מֵאֶרֶץ מִצְרָיִם. כִּי אִם חַי
יהוה אֲשֶׁר הֶעֱלָה אֶת־בְּנֵי יִשְׂרָאֵל מֵאֶרֶץ צָפוֹן וּמִכֹּל
הָאֲרָצוֹת אֲשֶׁר הִדִּיחָם שָׁמָּה, וַהֲשִׁבֹתִים עַל־אַדְמָתָם
אֲשֶׁר נָתַתִּי לַאֲבוֹתָם.

Assuredly, a time is coming—declares the Eternal—when it shall no more be said, "As the Eternal lives who brought the Israelites out of the land of Egypt," but rather "As the Eternal lives who brought the Israelites out of the north land, and out of all the lands into which they had been banished." For I will bring them back to their land, which I gave to their ancestors.
Jeremiah 16:14–15

The picture of Elijah's Cup is based on an ancient art form called micrography, where pictures are created using only letters. Can you sing or recite the entire song Eliyahu Hanavi *by following the stream of Hebrew letters in the illustration?*
Jeffrey Schrier

הִנֵּה אָנֹכִי שֹׁלֵחַ לָכֶם אֵת אֵלִיָּה הַנָּבִיא לִפְנֵי בּוֹא יוֹם יהוה הַגָּדוֹל וְהַנּוֹרָא. וְהֵשִׁיב לֵב־אָבוֹת עַל־בָּנִים וְלֵב בָּנִים עַל־אֲבוֹתָם.

Lo, I will send the prophet Elijah to you before the coming of the awesome, fearful day of the Eternal One, who will reconcile parents with children and children with parents. *Malaḥi 3:23*

Sing either Eliyahu Hanavi *or* Haraḥaman

אֵלִיָּהוּ הַנָּבִיא אֵלִיָּהוּ הַתִּשְׁבִּי אֵלִיָּהוּ הַגִּלְעָדִי. בִּמְהֵרָה בְיָמֵינוּ יָבֹא אֵלֵינוּ עִם מָשִׁיחַ בֶּן דָּוִד.

Eliyahu hanavi, Eliyahu hatishbi
Eliyahu, Eliyahu, Eliyahu hagiladi.
Bimherah veyameynu yavo eleynu
Im mashiaḥ ben David, im mashiaḥ ben David.

Elijah the prophet come speedily to us hailing messianic days.

הָרַחֲמָן הוּא יִשְׁלַח לָנוּ אֶת־אֵלִיָּהוּ הַנָּבִיא זָכוּר לַטּוֹב וִיבַשֶּׂר־לָנוּ בְּשׂוֹרוֹת טוֹבוֹת יְשׁוּעוֹת וְנֶחָמוֹת.

Haraḥaman hu yishlaḥ lanu et Eliyahu hanavi (2)
zaḥur latov. Vivaser lanu lanu (2) vivaser lanu besorot
tovot yishuot veneḥamot.

May the merciful One send us the prophet Elijah, of blessed memory, who will bring us good tidings, deliverance, and comfort.

Close the door.

HALLEL הלל

PSALMS OF PRAISE

The continuation of Hallel *follows. Traditional Pesaḥ songs begin on page 134.*

לֹא לָנוּ יהוה לֹא לָנוּ   כִּי לְשִׁמְךָ תֵּן כָּבוֹד
עַל חַסְדְּךָ עַל אֲמִתֶּךָ.
לָמָּה יֹאמְרוּ הַגּוֹיִם   אַיֵּה־נָא אֱלֹהֵיהֶם.
וֵאלֹהֵינוּ בַשָּׁמָיִם   כֹּל אֲשֶׁר חָפֵץ עָשָׂה.
עֲצַבֵּיהֶם כֶּסֶף וְזָהָב   מַעֲשֵׂה יְדֵי אָדָם.
פֶּה־לָהֶם וְלֹא יְדַבֵּרוּ   עֵינַיִם לָהֶם וְלֹא יִרְאוּ.
אָזְנַיִם לָהֶם וְלֹא יִשְׁמָעוּ   אַף לָהֶם וְלֹא יְרִיחוּן.
יְדֵיהֶם וְלֹא יְמִישׁוּן   רַגְלֵיהֶם וְלֹא יְהַלֵּכוּ
לֹא יֶהְגּוּ בִּגְרוֹנָם.
כְּמוֹהֶם יִהְיוּ עֹשֵׂיהֶם   כֹּל אֲשֶׁר־בֹּטֵחַ בָּהֶם.

Not for us, Eternal One; no, not for us,
but for your name: Bring forth a glorious event,
attesting to your love and to your truth!

Why should unbelievers say, "Where is their God?"
When our God is over us, and doing all according to desire!
Their preoccupations are with silver work and gold,
with works of human hands.

They have a mouth, but they can't speak.
They have eyes, but they can't see.
They have ears, but they can't hear.
They have a nose, but they can't smell.
They have their hands, but they can't feel.
They have their feet, but they can't walk.
They have nothing in their throats to say.
All that they make is just like them,
and all who trust in them.

יִשְׂרָאֵל בְּטַח בַּיהוה   עֶזְרָם וּמָגִנָּם הוּא.
בֵּית אַהֲרֹן בִּטְחוּ בַיהוה   עֶזְרָם וּמָגִנָּם הוּא.
יִרְאֵי יהוה בִּטְחוּ בַיהוה   עֶזְרָם וּמָגִנָּם הוּא.

Let Israel trust in The Eternal One,
who is their help and sheltering place.
Let the House of Aaron trust in The Eternal One,
who is their help and sheltering place.
Let all who fear The Eternal One trust in The Fount of Life,
who is their help and sheltering place.

Psalm 115:1–11

יהוה זְכָרָ֫נוּ יְבָרֵךְ   יְבָרֵךְ אֶת־בֵּית יִשְׂרָאֵל
יְבָרֵךְ אֶת־בֵּית אַהֲרֹן.
יְבָרֵךְ יִרְאֵי יהוה   הַקְּטַנִּים עִם־הַגְּדֹלִים.
יֹסֵף יהוה עֲלֵ֫יכֶם   עֲלֵ֫יכֶם וְעַל בְּנֵיכֶם.
בְּרוּכִים אַתֶּם לַיהוה   עֹשֵׂה שָׁמַ֫יִם וָאָ֫רֶץ.
הַשָּׁמַ֫יִם שָׁמַ֫יִם לַיהוה   וְהָאָ֫רֶץ נָתַן לִבְנֵי אָדָם.
לֹא הַמֵּתִים יְהַלְלוּ־יָהּ   וְלֹא כָּל־יֹרְדֵי דוּמָה.
וַאֲנַ֫חְנוּ נְבָרֵךְ יָהּ   מֵעַתָּה וְעַד עוֹלָם, הַלְלוּיָהּ.

Adonay zeḥaranu yevareḥ
Yevareḥ et beyt yisra'el yevareḥ et beyt aharon.
Yevareḥ yirey adonay haketanim im hagedolim.
Yosef adonay aleyḥem aleyḥem ve'al beneyḥem.
Beruḥim atem ladonay oseh shamayim va'aretz.
Hashamayim shamayim ladonay veha'aretz natan livney adam.
Lo hametim yehalelu yah velo kol yordey dumah.
Va'anaḥnu nevareḥ yah me'atah ve'ad olam
Halleluyah.

The Eternal One who has remembered us will bless us all
will bless the House of Israel,
will bless the House of Aaron,
will bless the ones in awe of The Eternal One,
young and old alike.

The Eternal One will add to you,
to you and to your children.
Blessed are you to The Eternal One,
to the maker of the heavens and the earth.
The skies are heaven, they belong to God,
the earth God gave for human life.
The dead cannot say "Halleluyah,"
none who have descended into stillness.
But we, the living, bless Yah's name,
today and forever, Halleluyah!

Psalm 115:12–18

אָהַבְתִּי כִּי־יִשְׁמַע יהוה אֶת־קוֹלִי תַּחֲנוּנָי.
כִּי־הִטָּה אָזְנוֹ לִי וּבְיָמַי אֶקְרָא.
אֲפָפוּנִי חֶבְלֵי־מָוֶת וּמְצָרֵי שְׁאוֹל מְצָאוּנִי
צָרָה וְיָגוֹן אֶמְצָא.
וּבְשֵׁם־יהוה אֶקְרָא אָנָּה, יהוה מַלְּטָה נַפְשִׁי.
חַנּוּן יהוה וְצַדִּיק וֵאלֹהֵינוּ מְרַחֵם.
שֹׁמֵר פְּתָאִים יהוה דַּלֹּתִי וְלִי יְהוֹשִׁיעַ.
שׁוּבִי נַפְשִׁי לִמְנוּחָיְכִי כִּי־יהוה גָּמַל עָלָיְכִי.

My love abounds, for God has heard
my voice, my plea for help.
God turns an ear to me,
while, in my days of trial, I call out.
The ropes of death have wrapped around me,
and in my trials Sheol itself has found me,
while I find pain and suffering.

And in the name of The Eternal One I call out:
"I pray, Eternal One, deliver me!"

Gracious is The Eternal One, truly just.
Our God is one who acts in tenderness.
The Eternal One protects those wandering in confusion,
I who feel so destitute, I, too, receive God's help.
Return, my soul, to your tranquility,
for The Eternal One has been generous with you!

כִּי חִלַּ֫צְתָּ נַפְשִׁי מִמָּ֫וֶת אֶת־עֵינִי מִן־דִּמְעָה
אֶת־רַגְלִי מִדֶּ֫חִי.
אֶתְהַלֵּךְ לִפְנֵי יהוה בְּאַרְצוֹת הַחַיִּים.
הֶאֱמַ֫נְתִּי כִּי אֲדַבֵּר אֲנִי עָנִ֫יתִי מְאֹד.
אֲנִי אָמַ֫רְתִּי בְחָפְזִי כָּל־הָאָדָם כֹּזֵב.

Truly, you released my soul from death,
my eye from tears, my foot from stumbling!

I walk about before The Eternal One,
to the world of life I have returned.

I am full of faith! For once I cried,
"How very desolate am I."

Once, in my alarm, I said,
"How false is everyone!"

Psalm 116:1–11

מָה־אָשִׁיב לַיהוה כָּל־תַּגְמוּלֹ֫והִי עָלָי.
כּוֹס־יְשׁוּעוֹת אֶשָּׂא וּבְשֵׁם יהוה אֶקְרָא.
נְדָרַי לַיהוה אֲשַׁלֵּם נֶגְדָה־נָּא לְכָל־עַמּוֹ.
יָקָר בְּעֵינֵי יהוה הַמָּ֫וְתָה לַחֲסִידָיו.

And now, what shall I give back to God?
For all God's bounties are upon me!

Salvation's cup I raise,
and in the name of The Eternal One, I call out.

My vow to The Eternal One I repay
here, I pray, before all those assembled here!

The Eternal One does not regard as trivial
the death of those who care for God.

אָֽנָּה יהוה כִּי־אֲנִי עַבְדֶּֽךָ אֲנִי־עַבְדְּךָ בֶּן־אֲמָתֶֽךָ
פִּתַּֽחְתָּ לְמוֹסֵרָֽי.
לְךָ־אֶזְבַּח זֶֽבַח תּוֹדָה וּבְשֵׁם יהוה אֶקְרָא.
נְדָרַי לַיהוה אֲשַׁלֵּם נֶגְדָה־נָּא לְכָל־עַמּוֹ.
בְּחַצְרוֹת בֵּית יהוה בְּתוֹכֵֽכִי יְרוּשָׁלָֽםִ הַלְלוּיָהּ.

Now, Eternal One, I am your servant.
I, your servant, child of your servant,
I whose fetters you have opened up.
To you I make my offering of thanks,
and in the name of The Eternal One I call out.
My vow to The Eternal One I repay
here, I pray, before all those assembled here
in courtyards of the House of God,
amid Jerusalem's most hallowed inner halls:
Halleluyah!

Psalm 116:12–19

הַלְלוּ אֶת־יהוה כָּל־גּוֹיִם שַׁבְּחֽוּהוּ כָּל־הָאֻמִּים.
כִּי גָבַר עָלֵֽינוּ חַסְדּוֹ וֶֽאֱמֶת־יהוה לְעוֹלָם הַלְלוּיָהּ.

Praise The Eternal One, all you nations,
all peoples, sing the praise of God!
For God's love overpowers us,
the truth of The Eternal One is forever.
Halleluyah!

Psalm 117

הוֹדוּ לַיהוה כִּי טוֹב — כִּי לְעוֹלָם חַסְדּוֹ.
יֹאמַר־נָא יִשְׂרָאֵל — כִּי לְעוֹלָם חַסְדּוֹ.
יֹאמְרוּ־נָא בֵית אַהֲרֹן — כִּי לְעוֹלָם חַסְדּוֹ.
יֹאמְרוּ־נָא יִרְאֵי יהוה — כִּי לְעוֹלָם חַסְדּוֹ.

Hodu ladonay ki tov — *Ki le'olam ḥasdo*
Yomar na yisra'el — *Ki le'olam ḥasdo*
Yomru na veyt aharon — *Ki le'olam ḥasdo*
Yomru na yirey adonay — *Ki le'olam ḥasdo.*

Give thanks to The Eternal One, who is good,
whose love is everlasting!
Let the Israelites declare today,
God's love is everlasting!
Let the House of Aaron say,
God's love is everlasting!
Let those in awe of God declare,
God's love is everlasting!

Psalm 118:1–4

מִן־הַמֵּצַר קָרָֽאתִי יָּהּ — עָנָֽנִי בַמֶּרְחַב יָהּ.
יהוה לִי לֹא אִירָא — מַה־יַּעֲשֶׂה לִי אָדָם.
יהוה לִי בְּעֹזְרָי — וַאֲנִי אֶרְאֶה בְשֹׂנְאָי.
טוֹב לַחֲסוֹת בַּיהוה — מִבְּטֹֽחַ בָּאָדָם.

Min hametzar karati yah anani vamerḥav yah.

From my distress, I cried out: "Yah!"
Yah answered, bringing great release.
The Eternal One is with me; I shall have no fear.
What can a human being do to me?
The Eternal One is with me, bringing help.
I gaze triumphantly upon my foes.
To trust in The Eternal One is good,
and surer than a trust in human power.

טוֹב לַחֲסוֹת בַּיהוה מִבְּטֹחַ בִּנְדִיבִים.
כָּל־גּוֹיִם סְבָבוּנִי בְּשֵׁם יהוה כִּי אֲמִילַם.
סַבּוּנִי גַם־סְבָבוּנִי בְּשֵׁם יהוה כִּי אֲמִילַם.
סַבּוּנִי כִדְבֹרִים דֹּעֲכוּ כְּאֵשׁ קוֹצִים
בְּשֵׁם יהוה כִּי אֲמִילַם.
דָּחֹה דְחִיתַנִי לִנְפֹּל וַיהוה עֲזָרָנִי.
עָזִּי וְזִמְרָת יָהּ וַיְהִי־לִי לִישׁוּעָה.
קוֹל רִנָּה וִישׁוּעָה בְּאָהֳלֵי צַדִּיקִים
יְמִין יהוה עֹשָׂה חָיִל.
יְמִין יהוה רוֹמֵמָה יְמִין יהוה עֹשָׂה חָיִל.

To trust in The Eternal One is good,
and surer than a trust in human benefactors.

All nations have surrounded me,
but with God's name I cut them off.

They surrounded me; yes, they surrounded me,
but with God's name I cut them off.

They surrounded me like swarming bees.
Like a brushfire, they were quenched,
and with God's name I cut them off.

You pushed me down, pushed me to fall,
but The Eternal One has brought help to me.

My strength, my song, is Yah,
who was for me a source of help.

The sound of song rejoicing in God's help
resounds amid the tents of all the just:
"The Eternal One's right hand delivers strength!
The Eternal One's right hand is lifted up,
The Eternal One's right hand delivers strength!"

לֹא אָמוּת כִּי אֶחְיֶה וַאֲסַפֵּר מַעֲשֵׂי יָהּ.
יַסֹּר יִסְּרַנִּי יָּהּ וְלַמָּוֶת לֹא נְתָנָנִי.
פִּתְחוּ־לִי שַׁעֲרֵי־צֶדֶק אָבֹא־בָם אוֹדֶה יָהּ.
זֶה־הַשַּׁעַר לַיהוה צַדִּיקִים יָבֹאוּ בוֹ.

Pitḥu li sha'arey tzedek avo vam odeh yah.
Zeh hasha'ar ladonay tzadikim yavo'u vo.

I shall not die, but I shall live,
and I shall tell the acts of Yah.

I truly have been tried by Yah,
but I was never given up to die.

Open to me, O you gateways of justice,
Yes, let me come in, and give thanks unto Yah!

This is the gateway to The Eternal One,
let all who are righteous come in.

Psalm 118:5–20

Chant each verse twice.

אוֹדְךָ כִּי עֲנִיתָנִי וַתְּהִי־לִי לִישׁוּעָה.
אֶבֶן מָאֲסוּ הַבּוֹנִים הָיְתָה לְרֹאשׁ פִּנָּה.
מֵאֵת יהוה הָיְתָה זֹּאת הִיא נִפְלָאת בְּעֵינֵינוּ.
זֶה־הַיּוֹם עָשָׂה יהוה נָגִילָה וְנִשְׂמְחָה בוֹ.

Odeḥa ki anitani vatehi li lishu'ah.
Even ma'asu habonim hayetah lerosh pinah.
Me'et adonay hayetah zot hi niflat be'eyneynu.
Zeh hayom asah adonay nagilah venismeḥah vo.

I give thanks to you, for you have answered me,
and have been to me a source of help.

The stone rejected by the builders,
has become this place's founding stone.

From The Eternal One this thing has come,
something wonderful, before our very eyes.

This very day, The Eternal One has acted.
Let us celebrate it, and express our joy.

Psalm 118:21–24

Chant responsively.

אָנָּא יהוה הוֹשִׁיעָה נָּא. אָנָּא יהוה הוֹשִׁיעָה נָּא.
אָנָּא יהוה הַצְלִיחָה נָּא. אָנָּא יהוה הַצְלִיחָה נָּא.

I pray, Abundant One, send us your help!
I pray, Abundant One, send us your help!
I pray, Abundant One, help us prevail!
I pray, Abundant One, help us prevail!

Psalm 118:25

בָּרוּךְ הַבָּא בְּשֵׁם יהוה בֵּרַכְנוּכֶם מִבֵּית יהוה.
אֵל יהוה וַיָּאֶר לָנוּ אִסְרוּ־חַג בַּעֲבֹתִים
עַד־קַרְנוֹת הַמִּזְבֵּחַ.
אֵלִי אַתָּה וְאוֹדֶךָּ אֱלֹהַי אֲרוֹמְמֶךָּ.
הוֹדוּ לַיהוה כִּי־טוֹב כִּי לְעוֹלָם חַסְדּוֹ.

Blessed all those who come in The Eternal One's name
we bless you in The Eternal One's house.

Divine is The Eternal One, who gives us light.

Adorn the festive place with leafy boughs,
up to the corners of the altar shrine.

You are my God; to you I offer thanks
my God, whom I revere.

Give thanks to The Eternal, who is good,
whose love is everlasting.

Psalm 118:26–29

This map reminds us of the delicate balance between oppression and freedom. Why do you think the base of ancient Israel is shown as matzah? Why is the map shown against a map of the Middle East that was created hundreds of years before Israel's independence? Postage stamps and cancellations pinpoint times in history that recall the difficult journey from oppression to freedom.
Jeffrey Schrier

34
70
SEPTENTRIO
Arama
TRACHONITIS
Astaroth
Cesarea Philippi
Enhazor
Bethsemes
Rama
Caldes
Capharnaum
Edrai
Tri.
CHA
Hamath
NANÆI.
Neptalim
Racotha
Aßor vel Hesron
G A
Rehuc
Harozeth
L I
Libanus
Mons
Hamon
GALILEA
SUPERIOR
SEU
GENTI
Speleà
Horma
Zephet
Cana
Bethemek
Sidon
Antilibanus mons
Acsaph
Saron
Tribus Aser
Montfort
Vallis Iephthael
INSURED
(VALEUR DÉCLARÉE)
Amead
PHOENI:
Bethdagon
Tyrus Sur nunc
Scandalium
Abdon
Acon
CIA
MARIS
Mare
34

ADIR HU • MIGHTY IS GOD

Adir hu, adir hu, yivneh veyto bekarov
bimheyrah bimheyrah beyameynu bekarov
El beney, el beney beney veyteḥa bekarov

Baḥur hu, gadol hu, dagul hu . . .
Hadur hu, vatik hu, zakay hu, ḥasid hu . . .
Tahor hu, yaḥid hu, kabir hu, lamud hu, meleḥ hu,
nora hu, sagiv hu, izuz hu, podeh hu, tzadik hu . . .
Kadosh hu, raḥum hu, shaday hu, takif hu . . .

Mighty is God, Mighty is God,
May the Temple be built immediately,
Swiftly, swiftly in our days.
O God build the Temple immediately.

Chosen is God
Great, renowned, glorious, faithful, just, pious, pure, unique, powerful, knowing, royal, awesome, exalted, potent, redeeming, righteous, holy, merciful, almighty, forceful.

אדיר הוא

אַדִּיר הוּא, יִבְנֶה בֵיתוֹ בְּקָרוֹב, בִּמְהֵרָה בִּמְהֵרָה, בְּיָמֵינוּ בְּקָרוֹב. אֵל בְּנֵה, אֵל בְּנֵה, בְּנֵה בֵיתְךָ בְּקָרוֹב.

בָּחוּר הוּא, גָּדוֹל הוּא, דָּגוּל הוּא, יִבְנֶה בֵיתוֹ בְּקָרוֹב, בִּמְהֵרָה בִּמְהֵרָה, בְּיָמֵינוּ בְּקָרוֹב. אֵל בְּנֵה, אֵל בְּנֵה, בְּנֵה בֵיתְךָ בְּקָרוֹב.

הָדוּר הוּא, וָתִיק הוּא, זַכַּאי הוּא, חָסִיד הוּא, יִבְנֶה בֵיתוֹ בְּקָרוֹב, בִּמְהֵרָה בִּמְהֵרָה, בְּיָמֵינוּ בְּקָרוֹב. אֵל בְּנֵה, אֵל בְּנֵה, בְּנֵה בֵיתְךָ בְּקָרוֹב.

טָהוֹר הוּא, יָחִיד הוּא, כַּבִּיר הוּא, לָמוּד הוּא, מֶלֶךְ הוּא, נוֹרָא הוּא, סַגִּיב הוּא, עִזּוּז הוּא, פּוֹדֶה הוּא, צַדִּיק הוּא, יִבְנֶה בֵיתוֹ בְּקָרוֹב, בִּמְהֵרָה בִּמְהֵרָה, בְּיָמֵינוּ בְּקָרוֹב. אֵל בְּנֵה, אֵל בְּנֵה, בְּנֵה בֵיתְךָ בְּקָרוֹב.

קָדוֹשׁ הוּא, רַחוּם הוּא, שַׁדַּי הוּא, תַּקִּיף הוּא, יִבְנֶה בֵיתוֹ בְּקָרוֹב, בִּמְהֵרָה בִּמְהֵרָה, בְּיָמֵינוּ בְּקָרוֹב. אֵל בְּנֵה, אֵל בְּנֵה, בְּנֵה בֵיתְךָ בְּקָרוֹב.

Religion speaks to heart and mind. As moderns, we want what we say and pray to reflect what we believe. The rational part of us demands consistency. But the emotional part of us understands that not all religious experience can be reduced to reason and logic.

For Reconstructionists, Hebrew prayer and song function to identify us with the Jewish people. We retain much of the traditional liturgy and, in this case, the traditional Pesaḥ table songs, as quotation rather than affirmation. The power of these songs is in the feelings they evoke rather than in the content they address.

When we sing, we associate ourselves with the Jews who crafted these songs out of their experiences, however removed from ours they may be. When we sing, we evoke memories of childhood and family when familiar melodies served as a bond and a celebration.

We should not forget that religion includes both play and playfulness; we need not always be engaged in serious ideological debate as to the meaning of tradition. Sometimes it is fine and fun to lean back, trade melodies, and sing the old "supernatural" songs—not because we believe the words but just because it feels good.
Richard Hirsh

KI LO NA'EH • PRAISE IS PROPER

Ki lo na'eh. Ki lo ya'eh.
Adir bimluḥah, baḥur kahalaḥah, gedudav yomru lo

leḥa uleḥa
leḥa ki leḥa
leḥa af leḥa
leḥa adonay hamamlaḥah
ki lo na'eh
ki lo ya'eh

Dagul bimluḥah, hadur kahalaḥah, vitikav yomru lo

leḥa u'leḥa
leḥa ki leḥa
leḥa af leḥa
leḥa adonay hamamlaḥah
ki lo na'eh
ki lo ya'eh

Zakay bimluḥah ḥasin kahalaḥah, tafserav yomru lo . . .
Yaḥid bimluḥah, kabir kahalaḥah, limudav yomru lo . . .
Moshel bimluḥah, nora kahalaḥah, sevivav yomru lo . . .
Anav bimluḥah, podeh kahalaḥah, tzadikav yomru lo . . .
Kadosh bimluḥah, raḥum kahalaḥah, shin'anav yomru lo . . .
Takif bimluḥah, tomeḥ kahalaḥah, temimav yomru lo . . .

For to God praise is proper, for to God praise is due.

Mighty and holy in sovereignty,
Truly chosen, truly merciful,
God's angelic hosts and human faithful proclaim
To you, only to you,
Yours is the sovereignty.
For to God praise is proper.
For to God praise is due.

כִּי לוֹ נָאֶה

כִּי לוֹ נָאֶה. כִּי לוֹ יָאֶה.

אַדִּיר בִּמְלוּכָה, בָּחוּר כַּהֲלָכָה, גְּדוּדָיו יֹאמְרוּ לוֹ:
לְךָ וּלְךָ, לְךָ כִּי לְךָ, לְךָ אַף לְךָ, לְךָ יהוה הַמַּמְלָכָה.
כִּי לוֹ נָאֶה, כִּי לוֹ יָאֶה.

דָּגוּל בִּמְלוּכָה, הָדוּר כַּהֲלָכָה, וְתִיקָיו יֹאמְרוּ לוֹ:
לְךָ וּלְךָ, לְךָ כִּי לְךָ, לְךָ אַף לְךָ, לְךָ יהוה הַמַּמְלָכָה.
כִּי לוֹ נָאֶה, כִּי לוֹ יָאֶה.

זַכַּאי בִּמְלוּכָה, חָסִין כַּהֲלָכָה, טַפְסְרָיו יֹאמְרוּ לוֹ:
לְךָ וּלְךָ, לְךָ כִּי לְךָ, לְךָ אַף לְךָ, לְךָ יהוה הַמַּמְלָכָה.
כִּי לוֹ נָאֶה, כִּי לוֹ יָאֶה.

יָחִיד בִּמְלוּכָה, כַּבִּיר כַּהֲלָכָה, לִמּוּדָיו יֹאמְרוּ לוֹ:
לְךָ וּלְךָ, לְךָ כִּי לְךָ, לְךָ אַף לְךָ, לְךָ יהוה הַמַּמְלָכָה.
כִּי לוֹ נָאֶה, כִּי לוֹ יָאֶה.

מוֹשֵׁל בִּמְלוּכָה, נוֹרָא כַּהֲלָכָה, סְבִיבָיו יֹאמְרוּ לוֹ:
לְךָ וּלְךָ, לְךָ כִּי לְךָ, לְךָ אַף לְךָ, לְךָ יהוה הַמַּמְלָכָה.
כִּי לוֹ נָאֶה, כִּי לוֹ יָאֶה.

עָנָיו בִּמְלוּכָה, פּוֹדֶה כַּהֲלָכָה, צַדִּיקָיו יֹאמְרוּ לוֹ:
לְךָ וּלְךָ, לְךָ כִּי לְךָ, לְךָ אַף לְךָ, לְךָ יהוה הַמַּמְלָכָה.
כִּי לוֹ נָאֶה, כִּי לוֹ יָאֶה.

קָדוֹשׁ בִּמְלוּכָה, רַחוּם כַּהֲלָכָה, שִׁנְאַנָּיו יֹאמְרוּ לוֹ:
לְךָ וּלְךָ, לְךָ כִּי לְךָ, לְךָ אַף לְךָ, לְךָ יהוה הַמַּמְלָכָה.
כִּי לוֹ נָאֶה, כִּי לוֹ יָאֶה.

תַּקִּיף בִּמְלוּכָה, תּוֹמֵךְ כַּהֲלָכָה, תְּמִימָיו יֹאמְרוּ לוֹ:
לְךָ וּלְךָ, לְךָ כִּי לְךָ, לְךָ אַף לְךָ, לְךָ יהוה הַמַּמְלָכָה.
כִּי לוֹ נָאֶה, כִּי לוֹ יָאֶה.

EḤAD MI YODEYA • WHO KNOWS ONE?

Eḥad mi yodeya? Eḥad ani yodeya.
Eḥad eloheynu shebashamayim uva'aretz.

Shenayim mi yodeya? Shenayim ani yodeya.
Sheney luḥot habrit, eḥad eloheynu shebashamayim uva'aretz.

Sheloshah mi yodeya? Sheloshah ani yodeya
Sheloshah avot, sheney luḥot habrit, eḥad eloheynu shebashamayim uva'aretz.

Arba mi yodeya? Arba ani yodeya.
Arba imahot, sheloshah avot . . .

Ḥamishah mi yodeya? Ḥamishah ani yodeya.
Ḥamishah ḥumshey torah, arba imahot . . .

Shishah mi yodeya? Shishah ani yodeya.
Shishah sidrey mishnah, ḥamishah ḥumshey torah . . .

Shivah mi yodeya? Shivah ani yodeya.
Shivah yemey shabata, shishah sidrey mishnah . . .

Shemonah mi yodeya? Shemonah ani yodeya.
Shemonah yemey milah, shivah yemey shabata . . .

Tishah mi yodeya? Tishah ani yodeya.
Tishah yarḥey ledah, shemonah yemey milah . . .

Asarah mi yodeya? Asarah ani yodeya.
Asarah dibraya, tishah yarḥey ledah . . .

Aḥad asar mi yodeya? Aḥad asar ani yodeya.
Aḥad asar koḥvaya, asarah dibraya . . .

Sheneym asar mi yodeya? Sheneym asar ani yodeya.
Sheneym asar shivtaya, aḥad asar koḥvaya . . .

Sheloshah asar mi yodeya? Sheloshah asar ani yodeya.
Sheloshah asar midaya, sheneym asar shivtaya . . .

אחד מי יודע

אֶחָד מִי יוֹדֵעַ? אֶחָד אֲנִי יוֹדֵעַ: אֶחָד אֱלֹהֵינוּ שֶׁבַּשָּׁמַיִם וּבָאָרֶץ.

שְׁנַיִם מִי יוֹדֵעַ? שְׁנַיִם אֲנִי יוֹדֵעַ: שְׁנֵי לֻחוֹת הַבְּרִית, אֶחָד אֱלֹהֵינוּ שֶׁבַּשָּׁמַיִם וּבָאָרֶץ.

שְׁלֹשָׁה מִי יוֹדֵעַ? שְׁלֹשָׁה אֲנִי יוֹדֵעַ: שְׁלֹשָׁה אָבוֹת, שְׁנֵי לֻחוֹת הַבְּרִית, אֶחָד אֱלֹהֵינוּ שֶׁבַּשָּׁמַיִם וּבָאָרֶץ.

אַרְבַּע מִי יוֹדֵעַ? אַרְבַּע אֲנִי יוֹדֵעַ: אַרְבַּע אִמָּהוֹת, שְׁלֹשָׁה אָבוֹת, שְׁנֵי לֻחוֹת הַבְּרִית, אֶחָד אֱלֹהֵינוּ שֶׁבַּשָּׁמַיִם וּבָאָרֶץ.

חֲמִשָּׁה מִי יוֹדֵעַ? חֲמִשָּׁה אֲנִי יוֹדֵעַ: חֲמִשָּׁה חֻמְשֵׁי תוֹרָה, אַרְבַּע אִמָּהוֹת, שְׁלֹשָׁה אָבוֹת, שְׁנֵי לֻחוֹת הַבְּרִית, אֶחָד אֱלֹהֵינוּ שֶׁבַּשָּׁמַיִם וּבָאָרֶץ.

שִׁשָּׁה מִי יוֹדֵעַ? שִׁשָּׁה אֲנִי יוֹדֵעַ: שִׁשָּׁה סִדְרֵי מִשְׁנָה, חֲמִשָּׁה חֻמְשֵׁי תוֹרָה, אַרְבַּע אִמָּהוֹת, שְׁלֹשָׁה אָבוֹת, שְׁנֵי לֻחוֹת הַבְּרִית, אֶחָד אֱלֹהֵינוּ שֶׁבַּשָּׁמַיִם וּבָאָרֶץ.

שִׁבְעָה מִי יוֹדֵעַ? שִׁבְעָה אֲנִי יוֹדֵעַ: שִׁבְעָה יְמֵי שַׁבַּתָּא, שִׁשָּׁה סִדְרֵי מִשְׁנָה, חֲמִשָּׁה חֻמְשֵׁי תוֹרָה, אַרְבַּע אִמָּהוֹת, שְׁלֹשָׁה אָבוֹת, שְׁנֵי לֻחוֹת הַבְּרִית, אֶחָד אֱלֹהֵינוּ שֶׁבַּשָּׁמַיִם וּבָאָרֶץ.

שְׁמוֹנָה מִי יוֹדֵעַ? שְׁמוֹנָה אֲנִי יוֹדֵעַ: שְׁמוֹנָה יְמֵי מִילָה, שִׁבְעָה יְמֵי שַׁבַּתָּא, שִׁשָּׁה סִדְרֵי מִשְׁנָה, חֲמִשָּׁה חֻמְשֵׁי תוֹרָה, אַרְבַּע אִמָּהוֹת, שְׁלֹשָׁה אָבוֹת, שְׁנֵי לֻחוֹת הַבְּרִית, אֶחָד אֱלֹהֵינוּ שֶׁבַּשָּׁמַיִם וּבָאָרֶץ.

תִּשְׁעָה מִי יוֹדֵעַ? תִּשְׁעָה אֲנִי יוֹדֵעַ: תִּשְׁעָה יַרְחֵי לֵדָה, שְׁמוֹנָה יְמֵי מִילָה, שִׁבְעָה יְמֵי שַׁבַּתָּא, שִׁשָּׁה סִדְרֵי מִשְׁנָה, חֲמִשָּׁה חֻמְשֵׁי תוֹרָה, אַרְבַּע אִמָּהוֹת, שְׁלֹשָׁה אָבוֹת, שְׁנֵי לֻחוֹת הַבְּרִית, אֶחָד אֱלֹהֵינוּ שֶׁבַּשָּׁמַיִם וּבָאָרֶץ.

Who knows one? I know one. One is our God in heaven and on earth.

Who knows two? I know two. Two are the tablets of the covenant. One is our God in heaven and on earth.

Who knows three? I know three. Three are our patriarchs. Two are the tablets of the covenant . . .

Who knows four? I know four. Four are our matriarchs. Three are . . .

Who knows five? I know five. Five are the books of the Torah. Four are . . .

Who knows six? I know six. Six are the orders of the Mishnah. Five are . . .

Who knows seven? I know seven. Seven are the days of the week. Six are . . .

Who knows eight? I know eight. Eight are the days to circumcision. Seven are . . .

Who knows nine? I know nine. Nine are the months to childbirth. Eight are . . .

Who knows ten? I know ten. Ten are the commandments of Sinai. Nine are . . .

Who knows eleven? I know eleven. Eleven are the stars of Joseph's dream. Ten are . . .

Who knows twelve? I know twelve. Twelve are the tribes of Israel. Eleven are . . .

Who knows thirteen? I know thirteen. Thirteen are the attributes of God. Twelve are . . .

עֲשָׂרָה מִי יוֹדֵעַ? עֲשָׂרָה אֲנִי יוֹדֵעַ: עֲשָׂרָה דִבְּרַיָּא, תִּשְׁעָה יַרְחֵי לֵדָה, שְׁמוֹנָה יְמֵי מִילָה, שִׁבְעָה יְמֵי שַׁבַּתָּא, שִׁשָּׁה סִדְרֵי מִשְׁנָה, חֲמִשָּׁה חֻמְשֵׁי תוֹרָה, אַרְבַּע אִמָּהוֹת, שְׁלשָׁה אָבוֹת, שְׁנֵי לֻחוֹת הַבְּרִית, אֶחָד אֱלֹהֵינוּ שֶׁבַּשָּׁמַיִם וּבָאָרֶץ.

אַחַד עָשָׂר מִי יוֹדֵעַ? אַחַד עָשָׂר אֲנִי יוֹדֵעַ: אַחַד עָשָׂר כּוֹכְבַיָּא, עֲשָׂרָה דִבְּרַיָּא, תִּשְׁעָה יַרְחֵי לֵדָה, שְׁמוֹנָה יְמֵי מִילָה, שִׁבְעָה יְמֵי שַׁבַּתָּא, שִׁשָּׁה סִדְרֵי מִשְׁנָה, חֲמִשָּׁה חֻמְשֵׁי תוֹרָה, אַרְבַּע אִמָּהוֹת, שְׁלשָׁה אָבוֹת, שְׁנֵי לֻחוֹת הַבְּרִית, אֶחָד אֱלֹהֵינוּ שֶׁבַּשָּׁמַיִם וּבָאָרֶץ.

שְׁנֵים עָשָׂר מִי יוֹדֵעַ? שְׁנֵים עָשָׂר אֲנִי יוֹדֵעַ: שְׁנֵים עָשָׂר שִׁבְטַיָּא, אַחַד עָשָׂר כּוֹכְבַיָּא, עֲשָׂרָה דִבְּרַיָּא, תִּשְׁעָה יַרְחֵי לֵדָה, שְׁמוֹנָה יְמֵי מִילָה, שִׁבְעָה יְמֵי שַׁבַּתָּא, שִׁשָּׁה סִדְרֵי מִשְׁנָה, חֲמִשָּׁה חֻמְשֵׁי תוֹרָה, אַרְבַּע אִמָּהוֹת, שְׁלשָׁה אָבוֹת, שְׁנֵי לֻחוֹת הַבְּרִית, אֶחָד אֱלֹהֵינוּ שֶׁבַּשָּׁמַיִם וּבָאָרֶץ.

שְׁלשָׁה עָשָׂר מִי יוֹדֵעַ? שְׁלשָׁה עָשָׂר אֲנִי יוֹדֵעַ: שְׁלשָׁה עָשָׂר מִדַּיָּא, שְׁנֵים עָשָׂר שִׁבְטַיָּא, אַחַד עָשָׂר כּוֹכְבַיָּא, עֲשָׂרָה דִבְּרַיָּא, תִּשְׁעָה יַרְחֵי לֵדָה, שְׁמוֹנָה יְמֵי מִילָה, שִׁבְעָה יְמֵי שַׁבַּתָּא, שִׁשָּׁה סִדְרֵי מִשְׁנָה, חֲמִשָּׁה חֻמְשֵׁי תוֹרָה, אַרְבַּע אִמָּהוֹת, שְׁלשָׁה אָבוֹת, שְׁנֵי לֻחוֹת הַבְּרִית, אֶחָד אֱלֹהֵינוּ שֶׁבַּשָּׁמַיִם וּבָאָרֶץ.

ḤAD GADYA • AN ONLY KID

Ḥad gadya ḥad gadya.
Dizvan aba bitrey zuzey, ḥad gadya ḥad gadya.

Va'ata shunra ve'aḥal legadya,
dizvan aba bitrey zuzey, ḥad gadya ḥad gadya.

Va'ata ḥalba venashaḥ leshunra, de'aḥal legadya, dizvan aba bitrey zuzey, ḥad gadya ḥad gadya.

Va'ata ḥutra vehikah leḥalba, denashaḥ leshunra, de'aḥal legadya, dizvan aba bitrey zuzey, ḥad gadya ḥad gadya.

Va'ata nura vesaraf leḥutra, dehikah leḥalba, denashaḥ leshunra, de'aḥal legadya, dizvan aba bitrey zuzey, ḥad gadya ḥad gadya.

Va'ata maya veḥavah lenura, desaraf leḥutra, dehikah leḥalba, denashaḥ leshunra, de'aḥal legadya, dizvan aba bitrey zuzey, ḥad gadya ḥad gadya.

Va'ata tora veshatah lemaya, deḥavah lenura, desaraf leḥutra, dehikah leḥalba, denashaḥ leshunra, de'aḥal legadya, dizvan aba bitrey zuzey, ḥad gadya ḥad gadya.

Va'ata hashoḥet veshaḥat letora, deshatah lemaya, deḥavah lenura, desaraf leḥutra, dehikah leḥalba, denashaḥ leshunra, de'aḥal legadya, dizvan aba bitrey zuzey, ḥad gadya ḥad gadya.

Va'ata malaḥ hamavet veshaḥat leshoḥet, deshaḥat letora, deshatah lemaya, deḥavah lenura, desaraf leḥutra, dehikah leḥalba, denashaḥ leshunra, de'aḥal legadya, dizvan aba bitrey zuzey, ḥad gadya ḥad gadya.

Va'ata hakadosh baruḥ hu veshaḥat lemalaḥ hamavet, deshaḥat leshoḥet, deshaḥat letora, deshatah lemaya, deḥavah lenura, desaraf leḥutra, dehikah leḥalba, denashaḥ leshunra, de'aḥal legadya, dizvan aba bitrey zuzey, ḥad gadya ḥad gadya.

חד גדיא

חַד גַּדְיָא חַד גַּדְיָא.
דִּזְבַן אַבָּא בִּתְרֵי זוּזֵי, חַד גַּדְיָא חַד גַּדְיָא.

וַאֲתָא שׁוּנְרָא וְאָכַל לְגַדְיָא, דִּזְבַן אַבָּא בִּתְרֵי זוּזֵי, חַד גַּדְיָא חַד גַּדְיָא.

וַאֲתָא כַלְבָּא וְנָשַׁךְ לְשׁוּנְרָא, דְּאָכַל לְגַדְיָא, דִּזְבַן אַבָּא בִּתְרֵי זוּזֵי, חַד גַּדְיָא חַד גַּדְיָא.

וַאֲתָא חוּטְרָא וְהִכָּה לְכַלְבָּא, דְּנָשַׁךְ לְשׁוּנְרָא, דְּאָכַל לְגַדְיָא, דִּזְבַן אַבָּא בִּתְרֵי זוּזֵי, חַד גַּדְיָא חַד גַּדְיָא.

וַאֲתָא נוּרָא וְשָׂרַף לְחוּטְרָא, דְּהִכָּה לְכַלְבָּא, דְּנָשַׁךְ לְשׁוּנְרָא, דְּאָכַל לְגַדְיָא, דִּזְבַן אַבָּא בִּתְרֵי זוּזֵי, חַד גַּדְיָא חַד גַּדְיָא.

וַאֲתָא מַיָּא וְכָבָה לְנוּרָא, דְּשָׂרַף לְחוּטְרָא, דְּהִכָּה לְכַלְבָּא, דְּנָשַׁךְ לְשׁוּנְרָא, דְּאָכַל לְגַדְיָא, דִּזְבַן אַבָּא בִּתְרֵי זוּזֵי, חַד גַּדְיָא חַד גַּדְיָא.

וַאֲתָא תוֹרָא וְשָׁתָה לְמַיָּא, דְּכָבָה לְנוּרָא, דְּשָׂרַף לְחוּטְרָא, דְּהִכָּה לְכַלְבָּא, דְּנָשַׁךְ לְשׁוּנְרָא, דְּאָכַל לְגַדְיָא, דִּזְבַן אַבָּא בִּתְרֵי זוּזֵי, חַד גַּדְיָא חַד גַּדְיָא.

וַאֲתָא הַשּׁוֹחֵט וְשָׁחַט לְתוֹרָא, דְּשָׁתָה לְמַיָּא, דְּכָבָה לְנוּרָא, דְּשָׂרַף לְחוּטְרָא, דְּהִכָּה לְכַלְבָּא, דְּנָשַׁךְ לְשׁוּנְרָא, דְּאָכַל לְגַדְיָא, דִּזְבַן אַבָּא בִּתְרֵי זוּזֵי, חַד גַּדְיָא חַד גַּדְיָא.

וַאֲתָא מַלְאַךְ הַמָּוֶת וְשָׁחַט לְשׁוֹחֵט, דְּשָׁחַט לְתוֹרָא, דְּשָׁתָה לְמַיָּא, דְּכָבָה לְנוּרָא, דְּשָׂרַף לְחוּטְרָא, דְּהִכָּה לְכַלְבָּא, דְּנָשַׁךְ לְשׁוּנְרָא, דְּאָכַל לְגַדְיָא, דִּזְבַן אַבָּא בִּתְרֵי זוּזֵי, חַד גַּדְיָא חַד גַּדְיָא.

וַאֲתָא הַקָּדוֹשׁ בָּרוּךְ הוּא וְשָׁחַט לְמַלְאַךְ הַמָּוֶת, דְּשָׁחַט לְשׁוֹחֵט, דְּשָׁחַט לְתוֹרָא, דְּשָׁתָה לְמַיָּא, דְּכָבָה לְנוּרָא, דְּשָׂרַף לְחוּטְרָא, דְּהִכָּה לְכַלְבָּא, דְּנָשַׁךְ לְשׁוּנְרָא, דְּאָכַל לְגַדְיָא, דִּזְבַן אַבָּא בִּתְרֵי זוּזֵי, חַד גַּדְיָא חַד גַּדְיָא.

An only kid, an only kid
My father bought for two zuzim, an only kid an only kid.

There came a cat and ate the kid my father bought for two zuzim. *Ḥad gadya, ḥad gadya.*

Then came a dog and bit the cat that ate the kid my father bought for two zuzim. *Ḥad gadya, ḥad gadya.*

Then came a stick and beat the dog that bit the cat that ate the kid my father bought for two zuzim. *Ḥad gadya, ḥad gadya.*

Then came a fire and burnt the stick that beat the dog that bit the cat that ate the kid my father bought for two zuzim. *Ḥad gadya, ḥad gadya.*

Then came water and quenched the fire that burnt the stick that beat the dog that bit the cat that ate the kid my father bought for two zuzim. *Ḥad gadya, ḥad gadya.*

Then came an ox and drank the water that quenched the fire that burnt the stick that beat the dog that bit the cat that ate the kid my father bought for two zuzim. *Ḥad gadya, ḥad gadya.*

Then came a slaughterer and killed the ox that drank the water that quenched the fire that burnt the stick that beat the dog that bit the cat that ate the kid my father bought for two zuzim. *Ḥad gadya, ḥad gadya.*

Then came the angel of death who killed the *shoḥet* who killed the ox that drank the water that quenched the fire that burnt the stick that beat the dog that bit the cat that ate the kid my father bought for two zuzim. *Ḥad gadya, ḥad gadya.*

Then came the Holy One and killed the angel of death who killed the *shoḥet* who killed the ox that drank the water that quenched the fire that burnt the stick that beat the dog that bit the cat that ate the kid my father bought for two zuzim. *Ḥad gadya, ḥad gadya.*

Singing either in English or in Hebrew, ask participants at the seder to each take a turn making the sound of the animal at the point in the song when that animal (or item) is mentioned. Once a person has made a particular sound, he or she repeats the sound each time the animal or item is sung. This can get pretty hilarious and enables even the youngest child to get involved. *Michael Strassfeld*

KAREV YOM • BRING US NEAR

Karev yom, karev yom, asher hu lo yom velo laylah (2)
Ram hoda hoda hoda ki leḥa hayom af leḥa halaylah.

Bring near that day that is not day or night.
Most High, announce that yours is the day and yours is the night.

קָרֵב יוֹם

קָרֵב יוֹם אֲשֶׁר הוּא לֹא יוֹם וְלֹא לַיְלָה,
רָם הוֹדַע כִּי לְךָ הַיּוֹם אַף לְךָ הַלַּיְלָה.

DODI LI • MY BELOVED IS MINE

Dodi li va'ani lo haro'eh bashoshanim.

Mi zot olah min hamidbar mi zot olah
mekuteret mor ulevonah.

Dodi li va'ani lo haro'eh bashoshanim.

Libavtini aḥoti kalah
libavtini kalah

Dodi li va'ani lo haro'eh bashoshanim.

Uri tzafon uvo'i teyman

Dodi li va'ani lo haro'eh bashoshanim.

My beloved is mine, and I am his, who browses in the lotus patch.

Who is this coming up out of the wilderness perfumed with myrrh and frankincense?

You have enlivened me, my sister-bride.

Awake, north wind, yes, come south wind!

(Selections from Song of Songs)

דּוֹדִי לִי

דּוֹדִי לִי וַאֲנִי לוֹ
הָרוֹעֶה בַּשּׁוֹשַׁנִּים.

מִי זֹאת עֹלָה מִן־הַמִּדְבָּר
מִי זֹאת עוֹלָה
מְקֻטֶּרֶת מוֹר וּלְבוֹנָה.

דּוֹדִי לִי וַאֲנִי לוֹ
הָרוֹעֶה בַּשּׁוֹשַׁנִּים.

לִבַּבְתִּנִי אֲחֹתִי כַּלָּה
לִבַּבְתִּינִי כַּלָּה.

דּוֹדִי לִי וַאֲנִי לוֹ
הָרוֹעֶה בַּשּׁוֹשַׁנִּים.

עוּרִי צָפוֹן וּבוֹאִי תֵימָן.

דּוֹדִי לִי וַאֲנִי לוֹ
הָרוֹעֶה בַּשּׁוֹשַׁנִּים.

NIRTZAH נרצה

CONCLUSION

Awareness, redemption, and gratitude accompanied our first three cups. This fourth cup is the cup of hope: Hope that next year we will all be free, that next year children and parents, neighbors and nations will turn their hearts to one another. Hope that next year Jerusalem will be a city of peace.

Lift the cup and recite:

בָּרוּךְ אַתָּה יהוה אֱלֹהֵינוּ מֶלֶךְ הָעוֹלָם בּוֹרֵא פְּרִי הַגָּפֶן.

Baruḥ atah adonay elo<u>hey</u>nu <u>me</u>leḥ ha'olam borey peri ha<u>ga</u>fen.

Blessed are you, Eternal One our God, sovereign of all worlds, who creates the fruit of the vine.

or

נְבָרֵךְ אֶת רוּחַ הָעוֹלָם בּוֹרֵאת פְּרִי הַגָּפֶן.

Nevareḥ et <u>ru</u>aḥ ha'olam boreyt peri ha<u>ga</u>fen.

We bless the spirit of the world, who creates the fruit of the vine.

In celebration, we add another blessing:

בָּרוּךְ אַתָּה יהוה אֱלֹהֵינוּ מֶלֶךְ הָעוֹלָם שֶׁעָשַׂנִי בֶּן/בַּת חוֹרִין.

Baruḥ atah adonay elo<u>hey</u>nu <u>me</u>leḥ ha'olam she'a<u>sa</u>ni ben/bat ḥorin.

Blessed are you, Eternal One our God, sovereign of all worlds, who has made me free.

or

נְבָרֵךְ אֶת רוּחַ הָעוֹלָם שֶׁעָשַׂנִי בֶּן/בַּת חוֹרִין.

Nevareḥ et <u>ru</u>aḥ ha'olam she'a<u>sa</u>ni ben/bat ḥorin.

We bless the spirit of the world, who has made me free.

Drink while reclining.

PASSOVER

Tell me: how is this night different
From all other nights?
How, tell me, is this Passover
Different from other Passovers?
Light the lamp, open the door wide
So the pilgrim can come in,
Gentile or Jew;
Under the rags perhaps the prophet is concealed.
Let him enter and sit down with us;
Let him listen, drink, sing and celebrate Passover;
Let him consume the bread of affliction,
The Pascal Lamb, sweet mortar and bitter herbs.
This is the night of differences
In which you lean your elbow on the table,
Since the forbidden becomes prescribed,
Evil is translated into good.
We spent the night recounting
Far-off events full of wonder,
And because of all the wine
The mountains will skip like rams.
Tonight they exchange questions:
The wise, the godless, the simple-minded and the child.
And time reverses its course,
Today flowing back into yesterday,
Like a river enclosed at its mouth.
Each of us has been a slave in Egypt,
Soaked straw and clay with sweat,
And crossed the sea dry-footed.
You too, stranger.
This year in fear and shame,
Next year in virtue and justice.

Primo Levi

After reading the poem, can you find the images in the illustration that remind you of the images in the poem?
Jeffrey Schrier

ל־אביב־יפו
עזה
פורט סעיד
אל־עריש
סואץ
ס י נ י
מ צ
מפרץ סואץ

In a world where Israel is just hours away by plane, this declaration requires more than a commitment to be in Jerusalem physically. It may be easier to have a seder in Israel next year than to bring Jerusalem into our lives every day.

As we prepare to leave our seder, we are reminded that redemption is two-fold: to join together as a people in a redeemed Jerusalem, and to be truly liberated wherever we are. We may have civil rights but be spiritual slaves. We may be enslaved to wrong ideas or to serving God out of fear, out of habit, and not out of love.

"I shall enter the heavenly Jerusalem," declared the Holy Blessed One, "only after my children enter Jerusalem on earth" (*Zohar* 1:1b). We set our sights on the year to come, to work tirelessly for the freedom that we have tasted with the matzah tonight.
Barbara Penzner

חֲסַל סִדּוּר פֶּֽסַח כְּהִלְכָתוֹ,
כְּכָל מִשְׁפָּטוֹ וְחֻקָּתוֹ.
כַּאֲשֶׁר זָכִֽינוּ לְסַדֵּר אוֹתוֹ,
כֵּן נִזְכֶּה לַעֲשׂוֹתוֹ.
זָךְ שׁוֹכֵן מְעוֹנָה,
קוֹמֵם קְהַל עֲדַת מִי מָנָה.
בְּקָרוֹב נַהֵל נִטְעֵי כַנָּה,
פְּדוּיִם לְצִיּוֹן בְּרִנָּה.

Now our seder is completed
Every requirement fulfilled.
Just as we have been privileged to observe it this year
may we continue to do so in years to come.

You who are pure, dwelling on high,
raise up your countless people.
Soon bring your offshoots strong
Redeemed to Zion in joyous song.

לַשָּׁנָה הַבָּאָה בִּירוּשָׁלָֽיִם.

Lashanah haba'ah birushalayim

Next year in Jerusalem!
Next year in a city of peace for all its inhabitants!

The Pesaḥ seder and Yom Kippur end on the same triumphant declaration: Next year in Jerusalem! On one side of the year, we are ending a day of fasting and introspection; on the other side, a feast and celebration. The spiritual cleansing of Yom Kippur makes us ready to listen, to care as individuals, to bring the messianic era closer. The physical cleansing and re-enactment of our enslavement remind us of our responsibility to make the world more ready for the messianic vision of justice and compassion. This credo represents the simple message that our job is not done—with freedom comes responsibility.
Naamah Kelman

ירושלים
Balfour reception
in Gymnasium Yard.
ISRAEL
BALFOUR
DECLARATION
ישראל
SNAKE PATH
MASADA
$ 5.-
467120
This card is yours. Keep it as a souvenir.
EL AL ISRAEL AIRLINES

APPENDIX I: THE PLAY

Narrator: These are the names of the sons of Israel who came to Egypt with Jacob—Reuben, Simon, Levi, Judah, Issaḥar, Zebulun, Benjamin, Dan, Naphtali, Gad, and Asher. The total number was seventy. Joseph was already in Egypt. The children of Israel multiplied and the land was full of them.

Announcer: Extra, extra—read all about it. New king in Egypt.

Hebrew I: I hope the new Pharaoh treats us as nicely as the other kings. I hope he remembers the things that Joseph did for Egypt many, many years ago.

Announcer: Extra, extra—read all about it. Pharaoh decides to make the Hebrews slaves. Pharaoh forces slaves to build cities.

Hebrew II: What got under his collar? What did we ever do to him? We're minding our own business and not bothering anybody. And boom! Just like that. He has us building cities.

Hebrew I: At least we don't have to build pyramids. Aren't they the most ridiculous looking things you've ever seen?

Pharaoh: Minister, come here.

Minister: Yes, great Pharaoh, ruler of Egypt, son of the sun god, master of the Nile. . . .

Pharaoh: All right, all right, enough already. What's the story with the Hebrew slaves?

Minister: They're still around.

Pharaoh: I know that. They're everywhere. They multiply like rabbits. The more work I give them, the more babies they have. We've got to get rid of them. Have you any ideas?

Minister: Why don't you let them go?

Pharaoh: That's a pretty stupid idea.

Minister: Maybe, if you asked them nicely, they'd stop having so many babies.

Pharaoh: You want me to ask them nicely to stop having babies? I'm the Pharaoh, ruler of Egypt, son of the sun god, master of the Nile. I don't ask anyone anything nicely. In fact, I don't ask. I act. I'd rather just kill them all.

Minister: Who would finish the cities?

Pharaoh: Drat, you're right. We'll have to do it slowly. We'll kill all the babies.

Minister: That could be awfully messy.

Pharaoh: All right. Just the male babies. Kill them as they are born. Have the boy babies thrown into the Nile.

Minister: But they'll drown.

Pharaoh: Bingo.

Narrator: A certain man of the house of Levi went and married a Levite woman. She bore a son and when she saw how beautiful he was, she hid him for three months. When she could care for him no longer, she put the child into a basket and placed him among the reeds of the Nile River.

Slave: Look, Princess. There's a basket floating down the river.

Princess: Pull it in and let's see what's inside. Oooh. A baby. Kitchy, kitchy koo. Where did he come from?

Slave: Probably from a mommy and daddy.

Princess: Most likely a Hebrew child. But I think I'll keep him. What shall I name him?

Slave: How about Basket, since that's what he's floating in?

Princess: Basket is a funny name.

Slave: What about Irving? You can call him Irving.

Princess: No, he shall be called Moses, for I drew him out of the water.

Slave: I like Irving better.

Narrator: Some time later, Moses grew up and went out to see the suffering of his Hebrew brothers and sisters. He saw an Egyptian beating a Hebrew. He looked around to see if anyone was looking. Then he struck down the Egyptian and hid him in the sand. The next day, Moses saw two Hebrews fighting.

Moses: Hey, there. Stop that.

Hebrew I: (mimicking) Hey there. Stop that. Who made you king? Mr. Big Shot. Mr. Fancy Shmancy Egyptian Prince. Are you going to kill me like you killed the Egyptian yesterday?

Moses: That's supposed to be a secret.

Hebrew II: Secret? It's all over the country. Your name is already on the most wanted tablets.

Moses: I've got to escape.

Narrator: Our top story tonight. After weeks of bloody water, frogs, swarming insects, pestilence, boils, and hail, Pharaoh has consented to meet once more with Moses and Aaron, leaders of the "Let My People Go Committee."

Moses: Pharaoh, let my people go. How long will you be hardhearted?

Minister: Pharaoh, perhaps you should listen to Moses.

Pharaoh: Nobody threatens the great Pharaoh.

Moses: "If you refuse to let my people go," says the Lord, God of the Hebrews, "I will bring locusts to your territory. What the hail didn't destroy, the locusts will eat. They'll eat everything from grain stalks to chin whiskers."

Pharaoh: You can't threaten me.

Minister: Oh great Pharaoh. We really didn't want locusts. There is no market for locusts. Lighten up, oh wondrous leader.

Pharaoh: Be gone from here, Hebrew nobodies.

Moses: Nobodies? My, my, my. We certainly are getting touchy.

Narrator: And locusts invaded the land of Egypt in a thick mass. They hid the land from view, for the land was covered with them. They ate all the grasses of the fields and the fruits of the trees so that nothing green remained in Egypt. And Pharaoh summoned Moses and Aaron.

Pharaoh: Friends, dear friends, pals, buddies.

Aaron: And now I suppose we should think he's serious. I don't trust him.

Pharaoh: Hey, I've sinned. I made a mistake. I stand guilty. Can you forgive me?

Moses: Will you let us go?

Pharaoh: Friend, pal, buddy. You scratch my back, I'll scratch yours, so to speak.

Moses: Very well. With a strong west wind God will lift the locusts from the land. Now, about your part of the bargain.

Pharaoh: Bargain? You're lucky to be alive. Scram, get out of here.

Aaron: I guess this means that you still won't let us go.

Pharaoh: Hey, who turned out the lights? Where did everyone go?

Minister: We seem to be having a blackout, Pharaoh.

Pharaoh: Ouch, you are standing on my foot. It's the middle of the day and I can't see one foot in front of my face.

Minister: Moses just pointed his staff towards the sky and suddenly there is this giant cloud of darkness.

Pharaoh: Moses again. Ow, you're sitting on my hand. That's it. Call Moses.

Moses: You rang?

Pharaoh: Get rid of the darkness and I'll let the slaves go.

Moses: This is the last time, Pharaoh. We and our cattle and our families and our possessions must be allowed to leave.

Pharaoh: Okay, okay.

Moses: There. The darkness is gone.

Pharaoh: Ah, there you are. Listen you, I will decide when and if you go. If I ever see you again, I shall kill you.

Moses: Pharaoh, you're right. You shall not see me again. But your people shall come begging that we be allowed to leave.

God: Moses, this is God.

Moses: Yes, God. I am here. What do we do next? The darkness was very effective. Pharaoh is going nuts. But he is one hardhearted fellow. Nine plagues haven't softened him.

God: It is time for the final plague, Moses. Are you ready?

Moses: Final? As in death?

God: Toward midnight, every firstborn in the land of Egypt shall die.

Aaron: We live in Egypt. Are we going to die, too?

God: Good question. This month shall be the first month of the year. We might as well start a calendar if you're going to be your own nation. On the tenth of the month, take a lamb and on the fourteenth, you shall sacrifice it and eat it roasted. You should be writing this down. Then take of its blood and mark the doorposts of your houses. Those homes with blood markings, I shall pass over.

Aaron: Pass over? What a great name for this night! Passover.

Moses: It is certainly better than Bloody Door Day.

God: This day shall be remembered always. Seven days you shall celebrate this event. No one shall eat leavened bread from the fourteenth to the twenty-first of this month. Now, I hope you remember everything I said. Go tell the people.

Narrator: In the middle of the night God struck down all the firstborn in the land of Egypt, from the firstborn of Pharaoh to the firstborn of the captive in the dungeon, and all the firstborn of the cattle. Pharaoh summoned Aaron and Moses in the middle of the night.

Pharaoh: Get out of here. Go. Leave us alone. *Adios. Au revoir. Sayanara.*

Aaron: Why, Moses—I do think that Pharaoh is letting our people go.

Moses: Now I think he's serious.

Narrator: The Hebrews left on foot in a hurry. About 600,000 plus children. And they baked unleavened bread in haste. The length of time that they lived in Egypt was 430 years. By strength of hand God brought us out of Egypt, out of the house of bondage.

Please turn to page 61 to continue the seder.

APPENDIX II: THE BIBLIODRAMA

Jewish tradition teaches that it is praiseworthy to expand upon the telling of the story of the Exodus. You might want to use the *Maggid* section of the seder to do something called bibliodrama, which involves speaking from *within* the text rather than speaking *about* the text. Below are a few suggestions for conducting a bibliodrama at the seder that will take approximately 30–40 minutes, depending on the number of participants and how involved they get in the role-playing. Children should be encouraged to take part in the drama as appropriate. As the leader, you will have a sense of which kinds of questions are most inviting to them. Following the guidelines below, you will find three scenarios you might wish to try, and some suggested questions for conducting your bibliodrama.

1. ***Introduction:*** Let people know that they will be doing something a little different. Instead of reading the text or talking about it, you will be inviting them to speak as characters within the text. In the bibliodrama, people will speak in the first person from within the story. For example, a person might say, "I'm Miriam. When I put my brother in the basket I whispered a silent prayer for his safety," rather than "I imagine Miriam was quite worried about her brother." Let people know that you welcome everybody's participation, though it is fine if some people wish merely to listen.

Although it is not essential, you may want to start by reading a small piece of the text you are using. In any case, be sure to give the background of the text in order to set the scene. For example, you might say, "You may remember that after the plagues, but before the actual exodus, there was a night of watching and attentiveness . . . " You can do this either by telling the story or by soliciting questions from participants.

2. ***Putting people in role:*** After a few minutes of introduction, you will need to move people into the scene itself. You will need to help them make the leap from the setting of the seder itself (the dining room, living room, or synagogue, for example), into the biblical setting. You might say, "I'd like you to take a moment now and imagine that instead of the person you are, you are actually an Israelite slave. If it helps you, close your eyes for a few seconds and imagine who you are, where you live, and what kind of work you do."

It is very important to give participants clear signals about where they are in the scene so they know how best to participate. As you continue to address them in character as "you," indicating who they are, you reinforce the magic of the drama. It is very common for people to revert back to speaking as they normally do: "I think they were probably terrified!" You need to gently bring them back: "So you are an Israelite slave? Are you feeling terrified?" Sometimes people will want to step outside the drama: "Can I ask a question. I'm not sure how the story actually goes." Try to bring them back into role or let them know you will have time to answer their question later but for now invite them to participate in the drama.

3. Some hints for encouraging participation: Ask inviting and open-ended questions: "You are waiting for a miracle. What is that like for you?" Avoid "yes" and "no" questions if you can. Try to reward people for their participation so they feel heard, appreciated, and part of the drama. You may do this by repeating or restating what a person said, especially if it clarifies something: "So, you are exhilarated! You just can't wait for what lies ahead." Make sure you are repeating more or less what the person meant. Sometimes you will just want to say "thank you," because what was said was powerful or too complicated to discuss or because you need to move on.

Remember, your main job as leader is host and interlocutor. Think of yourself as a wise and kind talk show host! You will keep the scene moving with your questions, your restatements, your active listening, and your gentle guidance from start to finish.

4. Leaving roles and "post-game" analysis: About ten minutes before you want the drama to end, you should begin to bring it to a close. You can do this in several ways: "I wonder who might like to offer one or two sentences about what you want future generations to know you are feeling at this moment?" Or: "As you look ahead, across the sea, back at Egypt, what is one thing you want to remember about this moment?"

To finish off the scene and move into a brief discussion and period of reflection, you need to bring people back to "real time." Sometimes it is enough to thank people for their willingness to be spontaneous and invite them to return to being themselves. Other times you will want to be more explicit, asking people to get up and stretch, look around and notice they are in a living room, not the desert. Always thank people for playing. Take a few minutes to discuss the drama. Be careful not to let people get back into their roles—the drama is over.

SUGGESTED SCENES

Avadim Hayinu/We were Slaves: The Torah talks about Israelite slavery; the Haggadah tells us that we were slaves in Egypt. Think back to the time when you were a slave. What is it like for you? What is your job? What keeps you going? What is one thing about your life now that you never want to forget? What do you talk about with your family?

Leyl Shimurim / The Night of Watching: What does the scene in your house look like? Who is there? What are you doing, and what are you talking about? What are the two things you must bring with you as you pack for the journey to freedom? What are you feeling? Do you have confidence in this guy Moses? In God? What is it like eating the lamb with your family?

Kriat Yam Suf / Crossing the Sea of Reeds: You are running toward the edge of the Sea. What are you thinking as you approach the water? What do you see around you? Who is with you? Do you think you will actually be able to cross to the other side? What makes you afraid? What gives you strength?

Susan Fendrick

Please turn to page 61 to continue the seder.

EDITORS

Joy Levitt is the Senior Program Director of the Jewish Community Center on the Upper West Side in Manhattan and was formerly a rabbi at the Reconstructionist Synagogue of the North Shore. She is the editor of *From Darkness to Light: A Passover Haggadah,* published by Ma'yan, the Jewish Women's Project of the Jewish Community Center on the Upper West Side and co-editor of *A Guide to Everything Jewish in New York* (Adama Books).

Michael Strassfeld is the rabbi of Congregation Ansche Chesed in Manhattan. He is the co-editor of the *Jewish Catalog* (Volumes I, II, and III: The Jewish Publication Society) and the author of *The Jewish Holidays: A Guide and Commentary* (Harper & Row). He is the editor of *A Passover Haggadah* (The Rabbinical Assembly). He is currently working on *The New Jewish Catalog: A Guide to Judaism as a Spiritual Practice,* to be published by Schocken Books.

ARTIST

Jeffrey Schrier is an internationally published artist whose work has been shown in museums throughout the United States and Europe. He is the artist/author of *On the Wings of Eagles: An Ethiopian Boy's Story* (Millbrook Press) and is currently working with tens of thousands of students nationally on "Wings of Witness," a Holocaust memorial made by transforming eleven million soda can tabs into a massive pair of wings.

DESIGNER

Adrianne Onderdonk Dudden has designed books and book jackets for publishers all around the United States. They include the *Jewish Catalogs, Tanakh: The Holy Scriptures, The Big Book of Jewish Humor,* the five volume *JPS Torah Commentary,* and the *JPS Hebrew-English Tanakh.* She is currently at work on a single volume *Ḥumash* and a new translation to the *Zohar.*

ABOUT THE ART Jeffrey Schrier's collages reflect his interest in meshing high technology and ancient subject matter by mixing laser prints with his drawings, memorabilia, maps, photos, and paint. Schrier's comments that accompany many of the illustrations in *A Night of Questions* were developed as he created the works of art. Memorabilia was generously supplied by the Sol Gluck collection.

COMMENTATORS

Sylvia Boorstein is a founding teacher of Spirit Rock Meditation Center in Woodacre, California. She lectures, writes, and teaches widely on the subject of living a mindful Jewish life.

Michael Cohen is Rabbi of Israel Congregation in Manchester Center, Vermont.

Tamara Cohen is Program Director of Ma'yan, The Jewish Women's Project of the Jewish Community Center on the Upper West Side, in New York.

Ira Eisenstein is President Emeritus of the Reconstructionist Rabbinical College.

Susan Fendrick is Rabbi-in-Residence at Jewish Family & Life.

Robert Goldenberg is Professor of History and Judaic Studies at the State University of New York at Stony Brook.

Arthur Green is Philip W. Lown Professor of Jewish Thought at Brandeis University and the former President of the Reconstructionist Rabbinical College.

Richard Hirsh is Executive Director of the Reconstructionist Rabbinical Association and the editor of *The Reconstructionist Journal.*

Naamah Kelman is Director of Educational Initiatives at the Hebrew Union College-Jewish Institute of Religion in Jerusalem.

Lori Lefkovitz is Director of Kolot: The Center for Jewish Women's and Gender Studies of the Reconstructionist Rabbinical College.

Barbara Penzner is Rabbi of Temple Hillel B'nai Torah in West Roxbury, Massachusetts.

Sandy Eisenberg Sasso is Rabbi of Congregation Beth El Zedek in Indianapolis, Indiana.

Jeffrey Schein is Director of Family Education Programs / Me'ah Director at the Cleveland College of Jewish Studies and Director of Education for the Jewish Reconstructionist Federation.

Toba Spitzer is Rabbi of Congregation Dorshei Tzedek in West Newton, Massachusetts.

David Teutsch is President of the Reconstructionist Rabbinical College.

Sheila Peltz Weinberg is Rabbi of the Jewish Community of Amherst, Massachusetts.

SOURCES AND PERMISSIONS

Hebrew texts that were previously translated by Joel Rosenberg for *Kol Haneshamah* (Reconstructionist Press) have been adapted for *A Night of Questions.* Other biblical texts have been adapted from *Tanakh: The Holy Scriptures,* published by the Jewish Publication Society. The "Grace After Meals" was translated by Zalman Schachter Shalomi and adapted by David Teutsch. All other translations were done by the editors. The editors acknowledge the ground-breaking work done by Marcia Falk in *The Book of Blessings* (HarperCollins), which provided inspiration for the new blessings used here. The editors further wish to acknowledge the previous *Haggadot* each of them developed, from which material and ideas were drawn: *A Passover Haggadah,* edited by Michael Strassfeld (Conservative Judaism, Volume XXXII, Number 3, Spring 1979) and *From Darkness to Light,* edited by Joy Levitt (Ma'yan, The Jewish Women's Project of the Jewish Community Center on the Upper West Side, 1994).

SOURCES

Page 53, 61. "Listen King Pharaoh," "Building Cities," and "The Frog Song" from *Passover Music Box,* words and music by Shirley Cohen, 1951, Kinor Records.

Page 86. Desmond Tutu, from *Hope and Suffering,* Skotaville Publishers, South Africa; William B. Eerdmans Publishing Co., USA, 1983.

Page 86. Franz Rosenzweig, in *Franz Rosenzweig: His Life and Thought,* presented by Nahum Glatzer, Schocken Books, 1970.

Page 87. Michael Walzer, *Exodus and Liberation,* Basic Books, 1986.

Page 106. Elie Wiesel, in *Legends of Our Time,* Schocken Books, 1982.

Page 109. Emma Lazarus, "The New Colossus," in *Emma Lazarus: Selections from her Poetry and Prose,* edited by Morris U. Schappes, published by the editor, 1982.

Page 111. Zelig Kalmanovitsch, excerpted from *The Literature of Destruction: Jewish Responses to Catastrophe,* edited by David Roskies, Jewish Publication Society, 1989.

Page 111. Nahum Glatzer, *The Language of Prayer,* Schocken Books, 1967.

Page 112. Mordechai Anielevitch, in *Anthology of Holocaust Literature,* edited by Jacob Glatstein, I. Knox, S. Margoshes, Jewish Publication Society, 1969.

Page 114. Muki Tzur, in *The Seventh Day: Soldiers Talk about the Six-Day War,* edited by Avraham Shapira, Charles Scribner's Sons, 1970.

Page 115. Raymonda Tawil, *My Home, My Prison,* Holt, Rinehart, and Winston, 1979.

PERMISSIONS

Page 40. *No Prayer is recited . . . ,* by Harold Schulweis. Reprinted by permission.

Page 40. *Some do not get the chance . . . ,* by Tamara Cohen, from *The Journey Continues,* Ma'yan, The Jewish Women's Project of the Jewish Community Center on the Upper West Side, 1997. Reprinted by permission.

Page 44. This excerpt from the book *Uncle Eli's Special-for-Kids, Most Fun Ever, Under-the-Table Passover Haggadah* (1-886411-26-3) appears courtesy of No Starch Press and is reproduced here by permission of the publisher.

Page 63. "Let My People Go," Simon & Schuster, Inc., and Artists and Writers, Inc., renewed 1981 by Simon & Schuster, Inc. Reprinted by permission.

Page 64. "Miriam's Song," music and lyrics by Debbie Friedman. Lyrics based on Exodus 15:20–21; published by Sound Write Productions, Inc. (ASCAP) © 1988. Reprinted by permission.

Page 65. "By the Shores," by G. Rayzel Robinson-Raphael. Reprinted by permission.

Page 67. "I Shall Sing to the Lord a New Song," by Ruth Sohn. Reprinted by permission.

Page 102. "Maggid," by Marge Piercy, in *Available Light,* © 1988 Middlemarsh, Inc., Reprinted by permission of Alfred A. Knopf, Inc.

Page 119. "Miriam Hanevi'ah," by Leila Gal Berner. Inspired by collaboration with Arthur Waskow. Originally published in *Or Chadash: Shabbat Morning Siddur,* P'nai Or Fellowship, 1987. Reprinted by permission.

Page 142. Primo Levi, "Passover," in *Collected Poems,* translated by Ruth Feldman and Brian Swan, Faber and Faber 1988. Reprinted by permission.

Pages 146–50. *The Play,* by Stan J. Beiner; reprinted with permission from *Sedra Scenes.* © A.R.E. Publishing, Inc., 1982.

PARTING THE WATERS: FOUR CUSTOMIZED SEDERS

Below are four suggested seder outlines for every age and stage. Feel free to adapt them to your own situation. You may find it helpful to make a copy of the outline you have chosen and keep it nearby during the seder.

SEDER 1: MORE IS MORE

Designed for adults and older children, this seder includes each of the elements of a traditional seder and tells the story of the Exodus using the biblical text as well as the questions of the Four Children and commentary. Its length is approximately one hour and thirty minutes before dinner.

27	The order of the seder
29	Introduction to the seder
31	*Kavanah*: *Kadesh* (blessing over wine or grape juice)
32–3	*Kadesh*
35	*Ureḥatz* (hand washing)
37	*Karpas* (dipping a vegetable in salt water)
40	*Yaḥatz* (breaking the middle matzah): choose one reading
41	*Ha laḥma anya* (This is the bread of affliction...)
	Yehi ratzon (May it be your will...)
	Comment by Arthur Green
42	*Kavanah*: Four Questions
43	Four Questions
46	*Avadim Hayinu* (We were slaves...)
	Song
47	*Miteḥilah* (From the beginning...)
50–1	Texts of the Four Children (with readings)
52	Biblical texts of the Exodus story
	Question of the wicked child
53	Biblical texts
	Question of the wise child
	Response to the wise child
54	Biblical text
	Question of the silent child
55	Biblical texts
58	Biblical text
	Question of the silent child
	Response to the silent child
59	Biblical texts
	Question of the challenging child
	Response to the challenging child
60	Biblical text
	Comment by Michael Strassfeld
61	Ten Plagues
	Questions of all four children
62	Biblical text
	Comment by Rabbi Naḥman of Bratzlav
63	Song: *Let My People Go*
	Biblical text
64–7	Choose one song or reading about Miriam
69	*Dayenu*
70	*Beḥol dor vador* (In every generation...)
	Lefihaḥ (Therefore...)
	Comment by Toba Spitzer
71	Song: *Venomar lefanav*
	Lefihaḥ (Therefore...)
72	Reading by Martin Luther King
73–4	*Hallel* (Psalms of praise)
76–7	Second Cup
79	*Roḥtzah* (hand washing)
	Comment by Jeffrey Schrier
80–1	*Motzi Matzah* (blessings over matzah)
82	Reading by Michael Strassfeld
83	*Maror* (blessing over bitter herbs)
84	Reading by Joy Levitt
85	*Koreḥ* (eating matzah and *maror* sandwich)
86	*Shulḥan Oreḥ* (the meal)

After the meal: see page 160

SEDER 2 LESS IS MORE

Intended for families with small children, this seder is structured to encourage parents and other adults present to engage children in the rituals and story of the Exodus. It makes use of the highlights of the Haggadah as well as commentary written for children and parents. It should take approximately forty-five minutes to complete before the meal.

After the meal: see page 160

SEDER 3 WE WERE ALL SLAVES IN EGYPT

Many people sitting around our seder tables have grown up in other religious traditions. This seder emphasizes the aspects inherent in the story of Pesah, drawing on the traditional text along with questions of the Four Children and It lasts approximately one hour and fifteen minutes before the meal.

After the meal: see page 160

...NG THE DOOR FOR MIRIAM

...music of the Haggadah that focuses on the role of women—past, present, and future—in the ... rituals using Miriam's Cup. For this seder, choose the second option when reciting ... approximately one hour and fifteen minutes before the meal.

niversal
ommentary.

...eder
...d Teutsch
...*sh* (blessing over wine or grape juice)

...t by Naamah Kelman
...*tz* (hand washing)
...mment by Naamah Kelman
...avanah: Karpas (dipping a vegetable in salt water)
Karpas
...0 *Yaḥatz* (breaking the middle matzah): choose one reading
41 *Ha laḥma anya* (This is the bread of affliction...)
Yehi ratzon (May it be your will...)
Comment by Arthur Green
42 *Kavanah*: Four Questions
43 Four Questions
Comment by Joy Levitt
46 *Avadim Hayinu* (We were slaves...)
Song
47 *Miteḥilah* (From the beginning...)
50–1 Texts of the Four Children (with readings)
151 Appendix Two: THE BIBLIODRAMA *or*
52 Biblical texts of the Exodus story
Comment by Toba Spitzer
Question of the wicked child
53 Biblical texts
Question of the wise child
54 Biblical text
Question of the silent child
55 Biblical texts
58 Biblical text
Question of the silent child
Response to the silent child
59 Biblical texts
Question of the simple child
Response to the simple child
60 Biblical text
61 Ten Plagues (If using the Bibliodrama, resume the seder here)
Questions of all four children
62 Biblical text
63 Song: *Let My People Go*
Biblical text
Comments by Sandy Eisenberg Sasso and Lori Lefkovitz
64–7 Songs and/or reading about Miriam
69 *Dayenu*
70 *Beḥol dor vador* (In every generation...)
Lefiḥah (Therefore...)
Comment by Toba Spitzer
71 Song: *Venomar lefanav*
Lefiḥah (Therefore...)
72 Reading by Martin Luther King
73–4 *Hallel* (Psalms of praise)
76–7 Second Cup
79 *Roḥtzah* (hand washing)
Comment by Jeffrey Schrier
80–1 *Motzi Matzah* (blessings over matzah)
82 Reading by Michael Strassfeld
83 *Maror* (blessing over bitter herbs)
84 Reading by Joy Levitt
85 *Koreḥ* (eating matzah and *maror* sandwich)
86 *Shulḥan Oreḥ* (the meal)

AFTER THE MEAL: The basics
89 *Tzafun* (eating the *afikoman*)
92/98 *Bareḥ* (blessings after the meal): choose one version
98 Third Cup
118–122 Cups of Miriam and Elijah
123–140 Selections from *Hallel* and Songs
141–144 Fourth Cup and conclusion

If you have more time, include the following:
100–117 *Beḥol dor vador* (In every generation...)
123–140 Additional selections from *Hallel* and Songs